SOFTWARE PATENTS

2002 Cumulative Supplement

SOFTWARE PATENTS
Second Edition

2002 Cumulative Supplement

Gregory A. Stobbs

Harness, Dickey & Pierce, P.L.C.

ASPEN LAW & BUSINESS
A Division of Aspen Publishers, Inc.
New York Gaithersburg

A Division of Aspen Publishers, Inc.
A Wolters Kluwer Company
www.aspenpublishers.com

Printed in the United States of America

1 2 3 4 5 6 7 8 9 0

Library of Congress Cataloging-in-Publication Data

Stobbs, Gregory A.
Software patents / Gregory A. Stobbs.—2nd ed.
p. cm.
Includes bibliographical references and index.
ISBN 0-7355-1499-2 (alk. paper)
ISBN 0-7355-2937-X (supplement)
1. Computer programs—United States—Patents. 2. Software protection—Law and legislation—United States. 3. Patent laws and legislation—United States. I. Title.

KF3133.C65 S76 2000
346.7304′86—dc21

00-031314

ABOUT ASPEN LAW & BUSINESS

Aspen Law & Business is a leading publisher of authoritative treatises, practice manuals, services, and journals for attorneys, corporate and bank directors, accountants, auditors, environmental compliance professionals, financial and tax advisors, and other business professionals. Our mission is to provide practical solution-based how-to information keyed to the latest original pronouncements, as well as the latest legislative, judicial, and regulatory developments.

We offer publications in the areas of accounting and auditing; antitrust; banking and finance; bankruptcy; business and commercial law; construction law; corporate law; criminal law; environmental compliance; government and administrative law; health law; insurance law; intellectual property; international law; legal practice and litigation; matrimonial and family law; pensions, benefits, and labor; real estate law; securities; and taxation.

Other Aspen Law & Business products treating intellectual property issues include:

Art Law Handbook
Business Method Patents
The Commercial Law of Intellectual Property
Copyright
Drafting Internet Agreements
Drafting License Agreements
Drafting Technology Patent License Agreements
E-Business Legal Handbook
E-Copyright Law Handbook
Epstein on Intellectual Property
Guide to Registering Trademarks
Handbook of Intellectual Property Claims and Remedies
Intellectual Property for the Internet
Intellectual Property Law Update
Intellectual Property Litigation: Pretrial Practice
Kohn on Music Licensing
The Law of Chemical and Pharmaceutical Invention
The Law of Internet Disputes
License Agreements: Forms and Checklists
Licensing Desk Book
Licensing Royalty Rates
Licensing Update
Patent Claim Construction
Patent Interference Practice Handbook
Patent Practice Handbook
Patent Technology Intelligence Report
Perle and Williams on Publishing Law
Protecting Trade Secrets, Patents, Copyrights, and Trademarks
Technology Transfer Guide
Trademark Counterfeiting
Trademark Law

ASPEN LAW & BUSINESS
A Division of Aspen Publishers, Inc.
A Wolters Kluwer Company
www.aspenpublishers.com

SUBSCRIPTION NOTICE

CONTENTS

SOFTWARE PATENTS

2002 Cumulative Supplement

CHAPTER 2

SOFTWARE TECHNOLOGY PRIMER FOR THE ATTORNEY

Page 75, add after end of § 2.07[E]:

§ 2.07 LARGE-SCALE SYSTEM DESIGN

[F] Large-Scale Client-Server Software Architectures

Client-Server architecture has become the de facto standard for constructing networked information systems, such as the Internet. As a result, the basic client-server approach has now been extended to several important large-scale architectures. It is important to have a basic understanding of these architectures if you are to ensure that your software patent claims will cover different implementations.

[1] Two-Tier Architectures

All current client-server architectures can be analyzed in terms of tiers. In its simplest form, client-server architecture can be implemented as a two-tier architecture made up of clients that talk directly to servers. Today, software engineers utilize the two-tier architecture when there are relatively few users in a work group, say on the order of 10 to 100 users. In a two-tier architecture, processing management is, by necessity, divided between client and server. Typically, processing management is spilt between the user interface environment of the client and the database management facilities of the server environment. As such, two-tier architectures are likely to be relatively inflexible when changes need to be made. It is difficult, for example, to move program functionality from one server technology to another without manually regenerating the procedural code.

Two-tier architectures also have difficulty managing session connectivity. Typically the server will bear responsibility for maintaining the connection with each client, so that the client can resume operation after a coffee break or other period of inactivity. To do this the server must periodically broadcast a "keep alive" message to each client. As the number of clients increases, these "keep alive" messages take a considerable toll on system performance. That is why two-tier architectures are best if kept below a few hundred users.

[2] Three-Tier Architectures

Software engineers developed three-tier architectures to overcome the inflexibility limitations of two-tier architectures. In a three-tier architecture there is a middle tier added between client and server. The software running on this middle tier is sometimes called "middleware." This middle tier can be used in a variety of ways. Software engineers will often recommend a three-tier architecture when there are a large number of users, say on the order of thousands of users. Processing management can be apportioned among the client tier, middle tier, and server tier in a variety of different ways. The middle tier can be designed to insulate client from server, so that changing from one server technology to another does not force changes in procedural code at the client tier. Also, the middle tier can be assigned the task of managing session connectivity. By moving the "keep alive" function to the middle tier, the burden on the server can be greatly reduced.

Software engineers have discovered how to use the middle tier in a variety of ways. Some will use the middle tier to perform queuing operations, or to execute applications, or to assemble database query results in a staging area for delivery to the client tier. A good way to analyze three-tier client-server architectures is to focus on what function the middle tier is performing. The following sections will present different three-tier architectures, each focusing on a different middleware function.

[a] Transaction-Processing Monitor Middleware

The middleware in this three-tier architecture performs a message queuing, transaction scheduling, or prioritizing function. The client connects to the middleware and hands it a request for information that the server will fill. The middleware then takes responsibility for contacting the server to obtain the requested information. This frees up the client to perform other tasks. When the middleware obtains the requested information it contacts the client and delivers the information. In the overall scheme of client-server middleware, the transaction-processing monitor is somewhat akin to the faithful lapdog that will fetch its master's newspaper on demand. To the middleware the information being passed between client and server is simply dumb data packets. The middleware layer is not designed to understand what the data packets contain.

[b] Message-Server Middleware

The message-server middleware takes the simple transaction-processing monitor middleware a step further. It acts as a go-between to facilitate communication between client and server. However, unlike the transaction-processing monitor, the message server understands something about what the data packets contain. Using this understanding, the message-server middleware can prioritize messages, delivering them asynchronously if desired. Unlike the faithful lapdog, the message-server middleware can go through the master's mail and pick out the important letters for delivery first.

[c] Application-Server Middleware

Before the application-server middleware was invented, client-server systems required the main body of an application to run on the client system. Usually the application would be run on the client side within the environment or operating system that provided the user interface. With the advent of server middleware, the main body of the application could be moved to a middleware server, leaving the client side responsible only for providing the user interface. Thus, the business logic, heavy number crunching, and data retrieval functions could be placed in a middle layer, out of harm's way of the desktop client. Application-server middleware techniques have made it possible to deploy and support applications across a large user base, without the cost, inconvenience, and security risk of installing individual copies of the application on each client desktop machine.

[d] Object-Request Broker Middleware

Taking the basic middleware concept to a higher level of abstraction, software engineers today are developing techniques to integrate object-oriented design in the client-server framework. Objects are software entities that contain not only data, but also the program code or methods that operate upon that data. The object-oriented paradigm offers a number of benefits that are discussed in § 2.05. Software engineers recognize that it would be highly desirable if the objects they develop could be distributed across a client-server environment. One way to do this is to employ an object-request broker as middleware to handle the distribution of software objects.

Developing robust object-request broker middleware is a considerably more complicated task than developing a simple message server or application server. There are several flavors of object-request broker middleware in popular use today. These include:

- CORBA (Common Object Request Broker Architecture),
- COM/DCOM (Component Object Model, Distributed Component Object Model), and
- Java RMI (Remote Method Invocation).

All three are popular standards and have faithful adherents. CORBA was developed by the Object Management Group (OMG). COM/DCOM is a Microsoft standard. Currently, Java RMI can be used only for Java-to-Java communication.

[e] Transactional-Component Middleware

Objects are now fairly well understood as software entities that contain both data and methods. Objects are often constructed to map onto real-world entities, such as employees and inventory items. The object-oriented paradigm gave software engineers a very powerful tool. It allowed them to devise objects for one application and then reuse them in another application.

Similar reuse techniques are being exploited in developing other types of abstractions called "components." A component is a program element (e.g., runtime code) that provides an interface allowing it to be "called" by another program element. The interface provides all needed information to allow other program elements to call and utilize it. The interface can be object-oriented, but it need not be. A Windows DLL is a component. It comprises a snippet of code designed to be reused and includes an application program interface by which a calling program can make use of that snippet of code. By comparison, FORTRAN programmers may recall the days when they wrote subroutines that could be called from another line in the program. These subroutines are not components, however. They lack the interface by which other programs can make use of their code.

Components are typically designed to work in one programming environment. A Windows DLL will work in the Windows operating system environment but not in the UNIX operating system environment. To use a component in a different programming environment it is necessary to know how that component must interface with the rest of the system. That is where transactional-component middleware comes in. Transactional-component middleware provides the instructions needed for a programming environment or platform to understand how to use the object in its environment.

Software engineers often use the term "container" when speaking of transactional-component middleware. In the Sun Microsystem Java world, components are sometimes called "java beans." To make the java beans useful across programming platforms they are placed in containers called "Enterprise Java Bean (EJB) Containers." In the Microsoft world components are called "COM objects,"and the containers are called "COM+ Containers." In the Microsoft approach, the underlying protocol is DCOM. An alternate protocol called "SOAP" for "Simple Object Access Protocol," has been proposed to allow client applications running on non-Microsoft platforms to access COM objects from a COM+ server. SOAP is a network protocol that uses XML data streams. It has been proposed as an Internet standard.

CHAPTER 5

SEARCHING FOR PRIOR ART

Page 256, add after end of § 5.09:

§ 5.10 SOFTWARE PRIOR ART SEARCHING

When *Software Patents* was initially written, the state of the software patent prior art was in turmoil. Issued software patents were often criticized as being of questionable validity, because, it was argued, the Patent Office did not have access to the best prior art. Some within the software community cried for the immediate abolition of all software patents, believing the Patent Office could never do a good job of examining software patents without access to the true prior art. Others counseled patience, arguing that the problem would gradually abate as the Patent Office's collection of prior art grew. Indeed, that collection of prior art has grown, but at a rate that has hardly been gradual. Software patents have been issuing like rabbits. Once scarce, now profuse — the collection of software art has seemingly changed overnight. The problem of finding the closest prior art remains, but the examiner's task has changed dramatically. Once there was nowhere to search, now there is everywhere.

This section addresses the new prior art, the software art that has issued since the software patent controversy of the mid 1990s began. It will attempt to explain how the new software art is classified today under the U.S. patent classification system. Before doing so, it may serve us well to have a better understanding of what the term "software" can encompass. As many engineers will tell you, software is in everything from dishwashers to satellite navigation systems.

[A] Defining the Term Software

What is software? Unfortunately, even noted lexicographers don't agree. While there are certainly common themes, the range of meaning covered by the term "software" is surprisingly broad. The following examples will illustrate:

In its on-line *Office 2000* dictionary, Microsoft defines software as "computer programs and applications, such as word processing or database packages, that can be run on a particular computer system." This definition seems to focus on software as package or product.

Merriam-Webster's Collegiate Dictionary defines software as "something used or associated with, and usually contrasted with hardware as: a) the entire set of programs, procedures, and related documentation associated with a system and especially a computer system, specifically: computer programs; b) materials for use with audiovisual equipment. This definition places a separation between hardware and software. Curiously, many engineers will tell you that the implementation in hardware versus software is largely a matter of design choice.

The American Heritage Dictionary of the English Language, Fourth Edition, defines "software" from a computer science perspective: Software "*Computer*

Science: The programs, routines, and symbolic languages that control the functioning of the hardware and direct its operation."[42]

Cambridge University recognizes at least two definitions: an English definition, and an American English definition. The English definition: "Software: the instructions which control what a computer does; computer programs. e.g., We are writing software to analyse the text."[43] The American English definition: "Software: the instructions that control what a computer can do; computer programs. e.g., educational software."[44]

The Random House Webster's College Dictionary reports even broader definitions: "Software: 1. a. programs for directing the operation of a computer or processing electronic data (as distinguished from *hardware*). b. documentation (def. 3).; 2. any material requiring the use of mechanical or electrical equipment, esp. audiovisual material such as film, tapes, or records."[45]

From the above examples, it is clear that the term "software" means many things to many people. From Microsoft's *Office 2000* perspective, software is a product. From Cambridge University's perspective, software is the instructions which control a computer. From the computer science perspective, as reported in the American Heritage Dictionary, software even includes symbolic language. Most of the definitions tie the term "software" to the domain of the computer: *computer* programs, directing the operation of a *computer,* instructions which control what a *computer* does. However, at least one definition, the Merriam Webster definition, suggests that the concept of "software" may extend beyond the bounds of *computer* to encompass *systems:* "the entire set of programs, procedures, and related documentation associated with a *system* and especially a computer system." The American Heritage definition that includes "symbolic languages" within the domain of software also supports view that software is more than merely fodder for computer.

Figure 5–6 illustrates how the above definitions overlap to define the term "software" with somewhat fuzzy boundaries. Depending on context, to define software as a product may be too restrictive, or not; to define software as symbolic language may be too expansive, or not. Depending on the context, a certain body of knowledge may be germane to defining what is the prior art; or that body of knowledge may be legitimately excluded as non-analogous art.

[B] Non-Analogous Art

The Patent Office instructs its examiners to discriminate between analogous and non-analogous art. The Manual of Patent Examining Procedure sets forth the following standard:

---

[42] American Heritage Dictionary of the English Language, 4th ed.

[43] Cambridge International Dictionary of English.

[44] Cambridge Dictionary of American English.

[45] Random House Webster's College Dictionary.

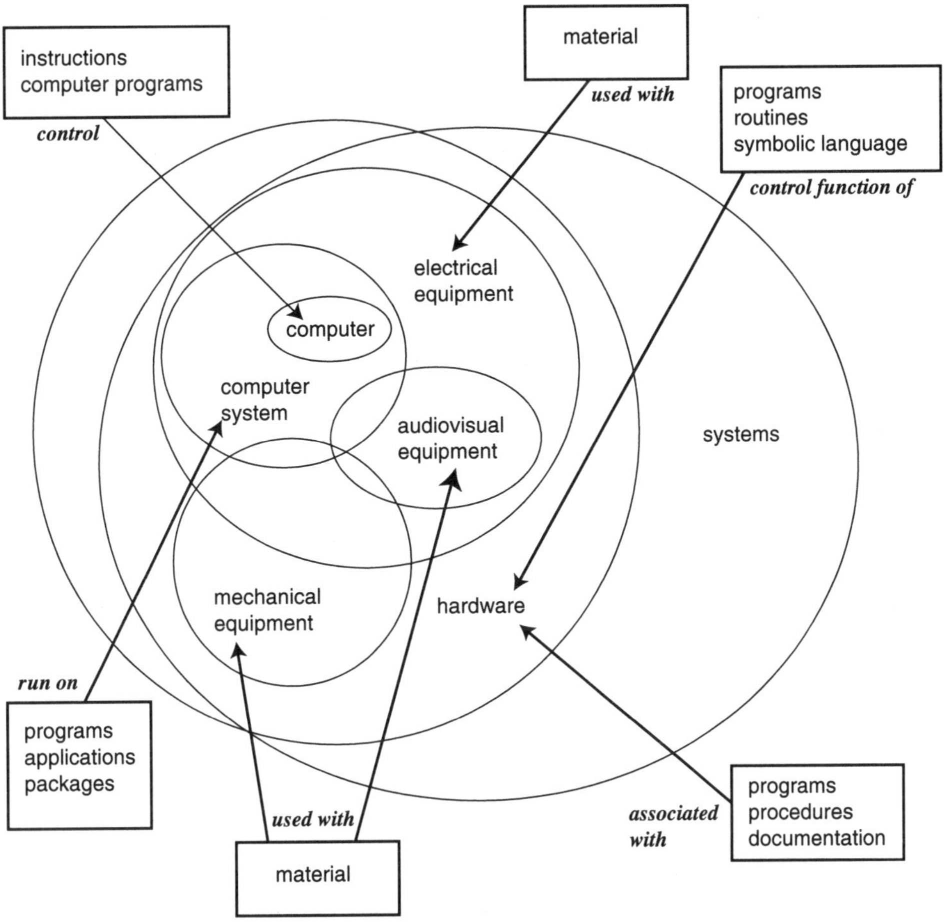

FIGURE 5–6. THE MANY DEFINITIONS OF SOFTWARE.

2141.01(a) Analogous and Nonanalogous Art

☞ **To rely on a reference under 35 U.S.C. §103, it must be analogous prior art.**

The examiner must determine what is "analogous prior art" for the purpose of analyzing the obviousness of the subject matter at issue. "In order to rely on a reference as a basis for rejection of an applicant's invention, the reference must either be in the field of applicant's endeavor or, if not, then be reasonably pertinent to the particular problem with which the inventor was concerned." *In re Oetiker,* 977 F.2d 1443, 1446, 24 U.S.P.Q.2d 1443, 1445 (Fed. Cir. 1992). See also *In re Deminski,* 796 F.2d 436, 230 U.S.P.Q. 313 (Fed. Cir. 1986); *In re Clay,* 966 F.2d 656, 659, 23 U.S.P.Q.2d 1058, 1060-61 (Fed. Cir. 1992) ("A reference is reasonably pertinent if, even though it may be in a different field from that of the inventor's endeavor, it is one which, because of the matter with which it deals, logically would have commended itself to an inventor's attention in considering his problem."); and *Wang*

Laboratories Inc. v. Toshiba Corp., 993 F.2d 858, 26 U.S.P.Q.2d 1767 (Fed. Cir. 1993).[46]

The Manual offers further assistance to the examiner in determining what art may be considered analogous. It suggests that the Patent Office classification of art may be relied upon as evidence of analogous art, but that similarities and differences in structure and function should carry more weight. Specifically, the Manual provides:

> ☞ **PTO classification is some evidence of analogy, but similarities and differences in structure and function carry more weight.**
>
> While Patent Office classification of references and the cross-references in the official search notes are some evidence of "nonanalogy" or "analogy" respectively, the court has found "the similarities and differences in structure and function of the inventions to carry far greater weight." *In re Ellis,* 476 F.2d 1370, 1372, 177 U.S.P.Q. 526, 527 (C.C.P.A. 1973).

As to inventions in the electrical arts, which presumably would apply to the software arts as well, the Manual offers the following advice as to how analogous art is to be considered:

> ☞ **Analogy in the electrical arts.**
>
> See, for example, Wang Laboratories, Inc. v. Toshiba Corp., 993 F.2d 858, 26 U.S.P.Q.2d 1767 (Fed. Cir. 1993) (Patent claims were directed to single in-line memory modules (SIMMs) for installation on a printed circuit mother-board for use in personal computers. Reference to a SIMM for an industrial controller was not necessarily in the same field of endeavor as the claimed subject matter merely because it related to memories. Reference was found to be in a different field of endeavor because it involved memory circuits in which modules of varying sizes may be added or replaced, whereas the claimed invention involved compact modular memories. Furthermore, since memory modules of the claims at issue were intended for personal computers and used dynamic random-access-memories, whereas reference SIMM was developed for use in large industrial machine controllers and only taught the use of static random-access-memories or read-only-memories, the finding that the reference was nonanalogous was supported by substantial evidence.); Medtronic, Inc. v. Cardiac Pacemakers, 721 F.2d 1563, 220 U.S.P.Q. 97 (Fed. Cir. 1983) (Patent claims were drawn to a cardiac pacemaker which comprised, among other components, a runaway inhibitor means for preventing a pacemaker malfunction from causing pulses to be applied at too high a frequency rate. Two references disclosed circuits used in high power, high frequency devices which inhibited the runaway of pulses from a pulse source. The court held that one of ordinary skill in the pacemaker designer art faced with a rate-limiting prob-

[46] Manual of Patent Examining Procedure, § 2141.01(a), 7th ed.

lem would look to the solutions of others faced with rate limiting problems, and therefore the references were in an analogous art.).[47]

Thus, in examining a software patent application for novelty and nonobviousness, the Patent Office instructs its examiners to look for prior art among bodies of knowledge that are accepted as being "reasonably pertinent" to the inventor's field of endeavor. The examiner is not restricted to the four corners of a given field of endeavor, but may draw analogy where similar structure or function may be found in other fields.

To illustrate, in the field of automated speech processing some of the basic understanding of human speech comes from a separate body of knowledge classified as "linguistics." Perusing the conference papers presented at recent symposia on automated speech recognition and synthesis, one can find examples illustrating that the linguistics has infused into automated speech processing (see Figure 5–7 for excerpts from Eurospeech '99). The full text of the syllabus may be found on the Internet by using any of a variety of search engines. Note that one of the keynote speakers and one of the presented papers have credentials that specifically include linguistics.

Thus an examiner reviewing a patent application for an automated method to extract meaning from syntactic content might wish to consult the writings of Noam Chomsky, such as *Aspects of the Theory of Syntax*[48] or *Syntactic Structures.*[49] Although these works are scholarly expositions on the nature of syntax in human language (not directed to computer software, per se) they present a deep understanding of syntax that computer software may be developed to reflect. Indeed, automated speech processing software may well employ data structures derived precisely from Chomsky's definitions of syntactic elements.

In contrast, the examiner would probably ignore works from the field of semiotics, the study of signs, symbols and "meaning," encompassing the study of signs such as animal cries, language disorders, medical symptoms, dictionary definitions and body language. Although books on semiotics may well rest on the linguist's bookshelf, next to books on syntactic theory, it is far less likely such books would rest on the bookshelf of the speech processing scientist. Thus Umberto Eco's seminal book, *Semiotics and the Philosophy of Language*[50] would likely fall outside the scope of the examiner's prior art investigation. That is not to say that this work is not of value to the study of linguistics. Rather, the work likely falls outside the scope of *present day* automated speech processing. As the field of automated speech processing advances, the field of semiotics may indeed fall within the scope of the analogous prior art. Thus, in defining the software patent

[47] Manual of Patent Examining Procedure, § 2141.01(a), 7th ed.

[48] Chomsky, N., Aspects of the Theory of Syntax, MIT Press 1965.

[49] Chomsky, N., Syntactic Structures (Annua Linguarum Series Minor 4, Series Volume 4, Peter Lang Publ. 1975).

[50] Eco, U. Semiotics and the Philosophy of Language, Indiana Univ. Press, 1986.

EUROSPEECH '99

Keynote Speeches

- Keynote Speech 1: Putting Language Into Language Modeling — Speaker: *Frederick Jelinek, Ciprian Chelba,* Center for Language and Speech Processing, USA
- Keynote Speech 2: The Controversial Connection Between Speech Production and Perception: Theories vs. Facts — *Speaker: Mária Gósy,* ***Research Institute for Linguistics,*** *Hungarian Academy of Sciences, Hungary*
- Keynote Speech 3: Multimedia Interaction for the New Millennium — *Speaker: Mark T. Maybury, Information Technology Division, The MITRE Corporation, USA*
- Keynote Speech 4: How Speech Works: Questions and Some Preliminary Answers — *Speaker: Björn Lindblom, Stockholm University, Sweden*
- Keynote Speech 5: Perspectives of Speech Technologies Research Highlighted in Eurospeech '99 — *Speaker: Hermann Ney, RWTH Aachen, Germany*

• • •

Speech Generation/Synthesis; Acoustic Synthesis & Units
Chair: Masanobu Abe, NTT Cyber Space Labs, Japan

- Sinusoidal Representation and Auditory Model-Based Parametric Matching and Smoothing and its Application in Speech Analysis/Synthesis — Au, O. C., Wan, W., Keung, C. L., Yim, C. H. *Hong Kong Uni. of Science and Technology, Hong Kong*
- Choose the Best to Modify the Least: A New-Generation Concatenative Synthesis System — Balestri, M., Pacchiotti, A., Quazza, S., Salza, P. L., Sandri, S. *CSELT S. p. A., Italy*
- Selection of Waveform Units for Corpus-Based Mandarin Speech Synthesis Based on Decision Trees and Prosodic Modification Costs — Chou, F.1, Tseng, C.1, Lee, L2 ***Inst. of Linguistics,*** *Academia Sinica, China; 2National Taiwan Uni., China*
- Improving Quality in a Speech Synthesizer Based on the MBROLA Algorithm — Etxebarria, B., Hernáez, I., Madariaga, I., Navas, E., Rodríguez, J. C., Gándara, R. *Uni. of the Basque Country, Spain*

• • •

FIGURE 5-7. EXCERPT FROM EUROSPEECH '99 SYMPOSIUM ON AUTOMATED SPEECH; SHOWING PARTICIPATION BY THE LINGUISTICS EXPERTS.

Speech Recognition; Adaptation

Chair: Jean-Claude Junqua, Panasonic Technologies, Inc. USA

- Prosodic Effects on Segmental Durations in Greek — Botinis, A.1, Fourakis, M.2, Prinou, I.3 *1Uni. of Skovde, Sweden; 2The Ohio State Uni., USA; 3Inst. for Language and Speech Proc., Greece*
- Within-Utterance Correlation for Speech Recognition — Blomberg, M. *KTH, Sweden*
- Techniques for Robust Speech Recognition in the Car Environment — Gelin, P., Junqua, J.-C. *Panasonic Technologies Inc., USA*
- An On-Line Acoustic Compensation Technique for Robust Speech Recognition — Giuliani, D. *ITC-IRST, Italy*

• • •

Speech and Noise-3

Chair: Jan Uhlir, Technical University of Prague,Czech Republic

- Channel Identification and Spectrum Estimation for Robust Automatic Speech Recognition — Zhao, Y. *Uni. of Missouri, USA*

FIGURE 5–7. *(continued)*

prior art, there is good reason to look beyond the restrictive domain of what is classically considered to be computer programs.

[C] Conducting a Prior Art Search — Defining the Scope of Search

Conducting a prior art search begins with defining the scope of the search. Just as in the previous speech processing example the field of search included linguistics but excluded semiotics, every prior art search will necessarily include certain bodies of knowledge and exclude others. Deciding what to include and what to exclude can be difficult, because it ultimately depends on the level of skill in a particular art. What bodies of knowledge are persons of skill in the art normally exposed to? What subjects are presented at conferences these persons attend? What books are on their bookshelves? These are some of the questions to ask in defining the scope of a prior art search. Of course, to answer these questions one must first grapple with the more fundamental question, who is one skilled in the art?

[1] Identifying One Skilled in the Art

One of ordinary skill in the art is a hypothetical person. That may seem surprising, inasmuch as inventors whose names appear on patents are real people and not hypothetical at all. However, as real people, each is an individual, with individual interests, intellect, upbringing, education, and life's experiences. No two inventors are alike, even in a well-defined field. What may be within the skill of one individual within that field may not be within the skill of another in that same field. Thus the person of "ordinary skill" is, of necessity, a legal fiction. It is an amalgam of the many persons who practice their craft in that field. If statistical analysis could be used to describe a legal fiction, the person of ordinary skill would probably fall under that famous bell-shaped curve. Excluded from that bell-shaped curve would fall, on the one extreme, a thousand monkeys randomly typing Shakespeare, and on the other extreme, the Einstein, Newton, Mozart geniuses to whom everything is obvious.

Regarding the 1,000 monkeys, one statistician has calculated that 1,000 monkeys seated at typewriters, for all practical purposes, will *never* type, "To be or not to be, that is the question." He calculates that even if one were to employ all monkeys in the known universe (17 billion galaxies, each containing 17 billion habitable planets, each planet with 17 billion monkeys) and set them typing away at a rate of one line per second for 17 billion years, the chances that all monkeys will fail is 99.999999999995%.[51] These numbers suggest that innovation is not a random act.

Thus it is unlikely the prior art searcher will ever need to explore the random acts of monkeys. On the other hand, most patent attorneys have encountered the overly erudite person to whom everything is obvious.

The U.S. Patent Office has promulgated its standard for defining who is one of ordinary skill in the art. Those standards, set forth in the Manual of Patent Examining Procedure at § 2141.03, are based on the case law. The Manual defines ordinary skill as follows.

[2] Manual of Patent Examining Procedure — Defines Ordinary Skill

The following is an excerpt of the pertinent section of the Manual of Patent Examining Procedure, describing how the Patent Office defines the level of ordinary skill.

> 2141.03 Level of Ordinary Skill in the Art
>
> FACTORS TO CONSIDER IN DETERMINING LEVEL OF ORDINARY SKILL
>
> "Factors that may be considered in determining level of ordinary skill in the art include (1) the educational level of the inventor; (2) type of problems encountered in the art; (3) prior art solutions to those problems; (4) rapidity

[51] <http://www.nutters.org/monkeys.html>.

with which innovations are made; (5) sophistication of the technology; and (6) educational level of active workers in the field." *Environmental Designs, Ltd. v. Union Oil Co.,* 713 F.2d 693, 696, 218 U.S.P.Q. 865, 868 (Fed. Cir. 1983), cert. denied, 464 U.S. 1043 (1984).

The "hypothetical 'person having ordinary skill in the art' to which the claimed subject matter pertains would, of necessity have the capability of understanding the scientific and engineering principles applicable to the pertinent art." *Ex parte Hiyamizu,* 10 U.S.P.Q.2d 1393, 1394 (Bd. Pat. App. & Inter. 1988) (The Board disagreed with the examiner's definition of one of ordinary skill in the art (a doctorate level engineer or scientist working at least 40 hours per week in semiconductor research or development), finding that the hypothetical person is not definable by way of credentials, and that the evidence in the application did not support the conclusion that such a person would require a doctorate or equivalent knowledge in science or engineering.).

References which do not qualify as prior art because they postdate the claimed invention may be relied upon to show the level of ordinary skill in the art at or around the time the invention was made. *Ex parte Erlich,* 22 U.S.P.Q. 1463 (Bd. Pat. App. & Inter. 1992).

SPECIFYING A PARTICULAR LEVEL OF SKILL IS NOT NECESSARY WHERE THE PRIOR ART ITSELF REFLECTS AN APPROPRIATE LEVEL

If the only facts of record pertaining to the level of skill in the art are found within the prior art of record, the court has held that an invention may be held to have been obvious without a specific finding of a particular level of skill where the prior art itself reflects an appropriate level. *Chore-Time Equipment, Inc. v. Cumberland Corp.,* 713 F.2d 774, 218 U.S.P.Q. 673 (Fed. Cir. 1983).

ASCERTAINING LEVEL OF ORDINARY SKILL IS NECESSARY TO MAINTAIN OBJECTIVITY

"The importance of resolving the level of ordinary skill in the art lies in the necessity of maintaining objectivity in the obviousness inquiry." *Ryko Mfg. Co. v. Nu-Star, Inc.,* 950 F.2d 714, 718, 21 U.S.P.Q.2d 1053, 1057 (Fed. Cir. 1991). The examiner must ascertain what would have been obvious to one of ordinary skill in the art at the time the invention was made, and not to the inventor, a judge, a lay-man, those skilled in remote arts, or to geniuses in the art at hand. *Environmental Designs, Ltd. v. Union Oil Co.,* 713 F.2d 693, 218 U.S.P.Q. 865 (Fed. Cir. 1983), cert. denied, 464 U.S. 1043 (1984).

[D] Planning the Field of Search

Whether one is conducting a prior art search as a precursor to filing a patent application, or as an assessment of validity of an issued patent, the steps are essentially the same. Begin by ascertaining the level of ordinary skill in the pertinent art and defining the field of search on that basis. Then devise a search methodology that allows you to systematically uncover and explore the art spanning your field of search. Finally, select the references that are potentially material to patentability, or that suggest leads for further exploration.

Getting started is often the most difficult part. An ill-conceived start may leave important prior art undiscovered, or may send one off to plow through material that ultimately proves barren. Ascertaining the level of ordinary skill and defining the field of search will often go hand in hand. As you investigate the level of ordinary skill you will discover resources to add to your field of search, and vice versa. Of course, previous experience with the particular art is invaluable — knowing where to look separates the successful from the unsuccessful.

So how do you assess the level of skill and devise your field of search when you have no prior experience with the particular art? A good place to begin is ask the experts. You may be fortunate to have access to experts in the field, such as the inventor for whom the patent application is being drafted, or the expert witness who will be testifying at trial. If so, ask these experts where they go to learn more about their field of expertise. Ask them to define who they think would be a person of ordinary skill in their art.

[1] Identifying Search Field Through Seminars and Symposia

If you do not have direct access to experts, you may nevertheless consult them through their writings. For example, say you are researching an invention that will monitor nightly news broadcasts to prepare synopses of selected news stories based on a user's pre-assigned preferences. One possible inventive aspect is how the system automatically extracts meaning from syntactic content of the stories. Instead of merely performing keyword spotting, the invention looks at the sentence structure and grammar used in the stories to gain understanding of what the stories mean.

While you could simply do a keyword search through the U.S. patent office web site — searching terms such as "syntax," "syntactic," "news," and "synopsis" — the results are likely to be quite hit-or-miss. A more powerful approach would be to first identify various communication channels through which the experts in this field exchange views with one another. One such channel might be conferences and symposia, and the technical papers presented at these. Trade publications represent another excellent channel. Each of these channels can be identified by conducting Internet searches.

What you are looking for is not necessarily the inventive concept, *per se*. Rather, you are looking for leads. What terminology do the experts use to describe the techniques involved in the invention? When you do perform keyword searches through published patent databases, these can be quite helpful in searching the keywords the experts are most likely to use. Who have authored papers in this field, and what companies or universities sponsor their work? Armed with this information you can conduct focused "inventor name" and "assignee" searches to discover if any key players have obtained patents in the field. For example, Figure 5–8

Chair: Philip C. Woodland, Cambridge University, UK

- The Philips/RWTH System for Transcription of Broadcast News — Beyerlein, P., et al. *Philips Research Labs., Germany*
- Toward Realtime Transcription of Broadcast News — Davenport, J., Nguyen, L., Matsoukas, S., Schwartz, R., Makhoul, J. *BBN Technologies, GTE Internetworking, USA*
- Recent Advances in Transcribing Television and Radio Broadcasts — Gauvain, J. - L., Lamel, L., Adda, G., Jardino, M. *LIMSI-CNRS, France*
- Selection for Acoustic Coverage from Unlimited Speech Data Extracted from Closed-Captioned TV — Jang, P. J., Hauptmann, A. G. *Carnegie Mellon Uni., USA*
- Laughter Extracted from Television Closed Captions as Speech Recognizer Training Data — Kennedy, P. E., Hauptmann, A. G. *Carnegie Mellon Uni., USA*
- Further Advances in Transcription of Broadcast News — Nguyen, L., et al. *BBN Technologies, GTE Corp., USA*
- Recent Advances in Japanese Broadcast News Transcription — Ohtsuki, K.1, Furui, S.2, Sakurai, N.2, Iwasaki, A.2, Zhang, Z. - P.2 *1NTT Cyber Space Labs., Japan; 2Tokyo Institute of Technology, Japan*
- Automatic Verification of Broadcast News Transcriptions — Pitz, M., Molau, S. *RWTH Aachen, Germany*
- Improved Speaker Segmentation and Segments Clustering Using the Bayesian Information Criterion — Tritschler, A., Gopinath, R. *IBM, Thomas J. Watson Research Center, USA*
- Development of the 1998 OGI-FONIX Broadcast News Transcription System — Wu, X., Yan, Y. *Oregon Graduate Institute, USA*
- Speech/Music Discrimination Based on Posterior Probability Features — Williams, G.1, Ellis, D. P. W.2 *1Uni. of Sheffield, UK; 2International Computer Science Institute, USA*
- Dragon Systems' 1998 Broadcast News Transcription System — Wegmann, S., Zhan, P., Carp, I., Newman, M., Yamron, J., Gillick, L. *Dragon Systems Inc., USA*
- Progress in Automatic Meeting Transcription — Yu, H., Finke, M., Waibel, A. *Carnegie Mellon Uni., USA*

FIGURE 5–8. RESULTS OF SEARCH ON SPEECH RECOGNITION IN BROADCAST NEWS.

shows an excerpt from the recent Eurospeech '99 symposium. Note, the symposium actually had a specific topic involving generating transcripts of broadcast news.

If you discover a particularly promising author, find out what else that author has written, and what other conferences or symposia the author has attended. If you discover a promising conference paper or article, check the bibliography to see if there are other even more promising articles. Also explore the co-authors. Sometimes co-authors work together regularly and may be involved in very similar work. You may find other pertinent papers written by one of the co-authors. Other times co-authors may have joined forces to publish this particular paper. They may come from more diverse backgrounds. Where there are co-authors, see if you can separate which authors are the more widely published from those who are relatively new to the field. The widely published authors may help you discover a broad spectrum of relevant articles, possibly with other co-authors.

[2] Ph.D. Theses

Interestingly, the newly published author may be an even more important find. If the newly published author is a recent Ph.D. graduate there is a good chance that his or her Ph.D. thesis will be relevant. Many companies hire recent Ph.D. graduates to boost their research and development expertise in growing technologies. Not infrequently, a newly hired Ph.D. graduate's work for the company will build upon or extend his or her Ph.D. thesis. A good resource for locating Ph.D. theses is through the UMI Company (formerly University Microfilm, Inc.).[52] The company maintains a web site at <www.umi.com> through which searches for recently published Ph.D. theses can be identified and obtained.

[3] Using Leads to Access the Issued Patent Collection

Once you have explored some of the seminars, symposia and technical papers, you are ready to construct a patent search. The U.S. Patent Office Web site at <www.uspto.gov/patft> provides an excellent search tool that may be accessed at no cost. One effective way to use this tool is through a series of separate searches, each designed to find the most pertinent prior art but coming from a different vantage point. A typical series of searches might include, for example:

- assignee searches — using companies, universities and institutions identified in the literature search to be active in the field;
- inventor name searches — using authors identified in the literature search;

[52] UMI Company, 300 North Zeeb Road, P.O. Box 1346, Ann Arbor, MI 48106. Phone: 800-521-0600; 313-761-4700. Fax: 313-761-9836. Website: <http://www.umi.com>.

- keyword searches — using terminology learned from the published literature;
- patent classification searches — using keywords as above but limited to specific patent classes and subclasses;
- pertinent patent searches — taking most pertinent patents and exploring both the prior art cited in those patents and also the later patents making reference to those patents.

[4] Identifying Appropriate U.S. Patent Classes and Subclasses

The patent classification search listed above presupposes that you know in which classes and subclasses to look. That can be a rather tall order. How do you know in which patent classes and subclasses to look? There are at least two techniques.

One is to discover the proper classes and subclasses by first finding at least one relevant patent and then identifying where that patent is classified (and if necessary, also finding what field of search the examiner used when the patent was examined). The first page of each issued patent identifies both where it is classified, and what field of search the examiner used during examination.

Another technique is to study the taxonomy or classification principles of the Patent Office Manual of Classification. In the software patent art, the classification system has grown quite complex. The Patent Office undertook a major reclassification campaign following the explosive growth in software patent filings in the mid-1990s. Hence, software patents are far better classified than they were in 1994. Subsection [E] below shows the state of the organization of the software patent classification system as of January 2001, and how it evolved from a simple subclass in the computer art, called "miscellaneous."

In most cases, a combination of both techniques may be used. To illustrate, using the example presented in § 5.10[D][1] above, we can use the list of authors names to search the Patent Office database for patents issued to those authors. Where a common name, such as Jones, Smith, Yu, or Wang is involved, we can limit the search further to the assignee that employed the person at the time the reference was published or some other keyword limitation. Figure 5–9 summarizes the results of such searches for the authors listed in the search results reproduced in Figure 5–8. Note that some of the patents identified specifically deal with the problem of transcribing broadcast news. See, for example, IBM patent 6,067,517 to Bahl, et al. (found by searching co-inventor/author Gopinath). The following is an excerpt from this patent. As a lead to finding prior art, this patent looks promising:

> Thus, the invention describes a technique to improve the recognition accuracy when **transcribing speech** data that contains data from a wide range of environments, as for example **broadcast news shows.**[53]

---

[53] U.S. patent 6,067,517 to Bahl, et al., issued May 23, 2000 and assigned to IBM.

Beyerlein

- 5,933,806 Method and system for pattern recognition based on dynamically constructing a subset of reference vectors
- 5,873,061 Method for constructing a model of a new word for addition to a word model database of a speech recognition system

Furui

- 5,835,890 Method for speaker adaptation of speech models recognition scheme using the method and recording medium having the speech recognition method recorded thereon
- 5,721,808 Method for the composition of noise-resistant hidden markov models for speech recognition and speech recognizer using the same

Gillick

- 6,167,377 Speech recognition language models
- 6,151,575 Rapid adaptation of speech models
- 6,052,657 Text segmentation and identification of topic using language models
- 6,029,124 Sequential, nonparametric speech recognition and speaker identification
- 5,946,654 Speaker identification using unsupervised speech models
- 5,822,730 Lexical tree pre-filtering in speech recognition
- 5,715,367 Apparatuses and methods for developing and using models for speech recognition
- 5,680,511 Systems and methods for word recognition
- 5,526,463 System for processing a succession of utterances spoken in continuous or discrete form

Gopinath

- 6,067,517 Transcription of speech data with segments from acoustically dissimilar environments
- 5,990,885 Personalized services, including a personal presence, for customers based upon collected personal preferences
- 5,751,905 Statistical acoustic processing method and apparatus for speech recognition using a toned phoneme system

Makhoul

- 5,933,525 Language-independent and segmentation-free optical character recognition system and method

FIGURE 5–9. AUTHOR SEARCH RESULTS.

Newman

- 6,151,575 Rapid adaptation of speech models
- 6,029,124 Sequential, nonparametric speech recognition and speaker identification
- 5,946,654 Speaker identification using unsupervised speech models

Nguyen

- 5,621,859 Single tree method for grammar directed, very large vocabulary speech recognizer

Sakurai

- 6,016,317 ATM cell switching system
- 5,995,510 Distributed type switching system
- 5,751,898 Speech recognition method and apparatus for use therein
- 5,748,850 Knowledge base system and recognition system
- 5,745,495 Apparatus for monitoring and controlling autonomous switching of trunk/subscriber lines in a distributed switching system
- 5,734,655 Distributed type switching system
- 5,732,394 Method and apparatus for word speech recognition by pattern matching
- 5,715,363 Method and apparatus for processing speech
- 5,684,841 Clocking converter for asynchronous data
- 5,621,849 Voice recognizing method and apparatus
- 5,586,172 Telephone exchange system
- 5,515,430 Volume controller
- 5,513,177 Distributed switching system having at least one module
- 5,506,713 Optical switching system
- 5,481,605 Private branch exchange capable of analyzing information received from ISDN

Waibel

- 5,855,000 Method and apparatus for correcting and repairing machine-transcribed input using independent or cross-modal secondary input
- 5,712,957 Locating and correcting erroneously recognized portions of utterances by rescoring based on two n-best lists

Yamron

- 6,052,657 Text segmentation and identification of topic using language models
- 5,680,511 Systems and methods for word recognition

FIGURE 5–9. *(continued)*

Yu

- 5,822,207 Apparatus and method for integrating intelligent manufacturing system with expert sheet metal planning and bending system
- 5,819,221 Speech recognition using clustered between word and/or phrase coarticulation
- 5,774,560 Digital acoustic reverberation filter network

Zhang

- 6,160,846 Apparatus and method for optimizing the rate control in a coding system
- 6,088,428 Voice controlled messaging system and processing method
- 6,084,908 Apparatus and method for quadtree based variable block size motion estimation
- 6,038,528 Robust speech processing with affine transform replicated data
- 5,982,165 RF circuit for use in a combined leakage detector and signal level monitor
- 5,960,387 Method and apparatus for compressing and decompressing a voice message in a voice messaging system
- 5,839,103 Speaker verification system using decision fusion logic
- 5,812,195 Video compression using an iterative correction data coding method and systems
- 5,802,208 Face recognition using DCT-based feature vectors
- 5,749,912 Low-cost, four-channel cochlear implant
- 5,649,086 System and method for parameter-based image synthesis using hierarchical networks
- 5,627,939 Speech recognition system and method employing data compression
- 5,610,657 Video compression using an iterative error data coding method
- 5,495,292 Inter-frame wavelet transform coder for color video compression

FIGURE 5–9. *(continued)*

According to the accompanying bibliographic information, the above IBM patent is classified in U.S. Patent Class 704, subclass 256 and cross-referenced in class 704, subclass 242. During examination, the examiner searched the following additional classes/subclasses:

> 395/2.44,2.52,2.53,2.86,2.4,2.79,2.6,2.64
> 704/235,236,243,244,245,251,252,255,256,257,277,276,270,278,200, 242,241.

The Patent Office maintains definitions on its Web site describing what each class and subclass contains. Class 704 is the primary class where speech recognition, speech synthesis, and language understanding systems are classified. The official designation for Class 704 is:

> Class 704: DATA PROCESSING: SPEECH SIGNAL PROCESSING, LINGUISTICS, LANGUAGE TRANSLATION, AND AUDIO COMPRESSION/DECOMPRESSION[54]

The primary and cross-referenced subclasses 256 and 242 assigned by the patent examiner in this case contain the following subject matter:

> 256 Markov:
> This subclass is indented under subclass 255. Subject matter wherein the models include states which represent speech sound portions and transitions which represent connections between speech sound portions (e.g., hidden Markov models, heuristic Markov models, etc.).
>
> 242 Viterbi Trellis:
> This subclass is indented under subclass 236. Subject matter wherein discrete components are distinguished by traversing possible paths through a time series.[55]

Who would have thought that Markov and Viterbi Trellis topics would have been relevant to our search for broadcast news translation. Maybe they're not. Before proceeding a sanity check is in order.

[a] Assessing Whether the Identified Subclass Is Pertinent

Before simply searching these subclasses for other examples of broadcast news transcription, it is wise to consider why the above-identified IBM patent was classified here. Patents are classified by the subject matter they *claim,* not by the subject matter they *disclose.* In this case, the claim was directed to the general problem of how to discriminate between speech and non-speech, such as background music, when performing a transcription. Claim 1 of that patent reads:

> 1. A method for transcribing a segment of data that includes speech in one or more environments and non-speech data, comprising:
>
> inputting the data to a segmenter and producing a series of segments, each segment being given a type identifier tag selected from a predetermined set of classes; and
>
> transcribing each type identifier tagged segment using a specific system created for that type.

[54] <www.uspto.gov/web/offices/ac/ido/oeip/taf/def/704.htm>.
[55] <www.uspto.gov/web/offices/ac/ido/oeip/taf/def/704.htm>.

The claimed subject matter is not necessarily the subject matter we are searching for, although the excerpt from the specification certainly seems pertinent. However, because patents are classified by claimed subject matter, we cannot be sure, from this one patent alone, that subclasses 242 and 256 are relevant to our present search. We can check to be sure that these subclasses are potentially relevant by running simple keyword searches in both. Access the U.S. Patent Office database via the Internet and enter the following searches:

CCL 704/242 AND news

CCL 704/256 AND news

These searches explore the current U.S. class/subclass (CCL) seeking patents containing the word "news." Both searches uncover patents dealing with the transcribing broadcast news, as Figure 5–10 shows.

Thus we can conclude that class 704 is certainly relevant, and that subclasses 242 and 256 are also potentially relevant. Of course, there may be other worthwhile subclasses within class 704. We can identify these by studying the classification taxonomy.

[b] Identifying Additional Subclasses by Taxonomy Study

With class 704 as the primary focal point, we can now examine the classification taxonomy to determine if there are other subclasses, besides 242 and 256

Searching All Years . . .

Results of Search in All Years db for:

CCL/704/256 AND news: 6 patents.

Hits **1** through **6** out of **6**

Jump To

Refine Search

	PAT. NO.	Title
1	6,185,531	Topic indexing method
2	6,076,056	Speech recognition system for recognizing continuous and isolated speech
3	6,067,520	System and method of recognizing continuous mandarin speech utilizing chinese hidden markou models
4	6,067,517	Transcription of speech data with segments from acoustically dissimilar environments
5	6,044,344	Constrained corrective training for continuous parameter system
6	5,884,259	Method and apparatus for a time-synchronous tree-based search strategy

FIGURE 5–10. SEARCH RESULTS.

that should be searched. The Patent Office usually groups related subject matter together, often in indented, outline form. Thus, if subclasses 242 and 256 are potentially relevant, the neighboring subclasses may also be potentially relevant.

In addition, it may also be helpful to look at the field of search used by the examiner in examining our identified patent. Although the examiner of the identified patent was searching for different claimed subject matter, the field of search could point us to additional places that may be worth searching. In this case, the examiner's field of search included the following subclasses from class 704: 235, 236, 243, 244, 245, 251, 252, 255, 256, 257, 277, 276, 270, 278, 200, 242, 241. In addition, the examiner also searched class 395, subclasses 2.44, 2.52, 2.53, 2.86, 2.4, 2.79, 2.6, 2.64. That means that these classes and subclasses could be potentially relevant.

Therefore, from our exploration thus far, we know we need to take a look at class 704, subclasses 242 and 256, and possibly all subclasses in the range from 200 to 278 (based on the examiner's field of search). In addition, we need to take a further look at class 395.

Does that mean we should now jump in and start searching all of these subclasses? We could, but there is one other thing to check. In addition to maintaining class listings and class definitions, such as the definitions of subclasses 242 and 256 reproduced above, the Manual of U.S. Patent Classification also includes valuable search notes. The Manual can be examined on-line at the U.S. Patent Office web site.[56] Figure 5–11 portrays an excerpt from the search notes for class 704. The notes tell us something about how the class evolved, how it is currently organized and whether there are any related classes worth taking a look at.

Armed with this information, let us take a look at the 704 class listing, focusing on the portion containing subclasses 242 and 256. The listing for subclasses 200 through 278 is reproduced in Figure 5–12. From the listing we can see that our two subclasses, as well as the subclasses included in the examiner's field of search, concentrate generally on speech processing and more particularly on recognition. Specifically, both subclasses 242 and 256 are children of the more general "recognition" subclass 231.

We can also take a look at class 395, which the examiner included in the field of search. A listing of that subclass as it existed in 1995 is shown in Figure 5–13.

You might be curious to know why the subclasses of class 395 appear to overlap with class 704. The answer lies in the annals of the ever-changing Patent Office classification system. Beginning in around 1997, the Patent Office began replacing class 395 with a new 700 series of classes. If fact, if you now consult the current Manual of Classification (at this writing, the December 1999 edition), you would find that the subclasses of class 395 listed above no longer exist. They were, in effect, moved to class 704 (Speech Processing).

---

[56] <www.uspto.gov/web/offices/ac/ido/oeip/taf/moc/index.htm>.

Class Definition

This is the generic class for apparatus and corresponding methods for constructing, analyzing, and modifying units of human language by data processing, in which there is a significant change in the data.

This class also provides for systems or methods that process speech signals for storage, transmission, recognition, or synthesis of speech.

This class also provides for systems or methods for bandwidth compression or expansion of an audio signal, or for time compression or expansion of an audio signal.

Class 704 is structured into three main divisions:

A. Linguistics.

B. Speech Signal Processing.

C. Audio Compression.

See Subclass References to the Current Class, below, for the subclasses located within each of these three main divisions.

LINES WITH OTHER CLASSES AND WITHIN THIS CLASS

A. LINGUISTICS

1. This class does not include subject matter wherein significant details of the modification or construction of documents are claimed. (See Class 707 in the Search Class notes below in References to Other Classes, regarding Document Processing).
2. This class does not include subject matter directed to significant details of teaching languages. (See Class 434 in the Search Class notes in References to Other Classes, below).
3. This class does not include subject matter directed to significant details of the construction, analysis or modification of computer languages. (See Class 395 in the Search Class notes in References to Other Classes, below).

B. IMAGE ANALYSIS

1. This class does not include subject matter wherein significant image analysis is performed and speech signal processing is nominally claimed (see Class 382 in the Search Class notes in References to Other Classes, below).
2. This class includes subject matter directed to speech signal processing disclosed or claimed in plural diverse arts such as image analysis (classified, per se, in Class 382).

FIGURE 5–11. EXCERPT FROM SEARCH NOTES FOR CLASS 704.

C. AUDIO SIGNAL PROCESSING

1. This class does not include subject matter wherein nominal bandwidth or time modifications are performed for other audio processing defined in Classes 381 or 84 (see Search Class notes below in References to Other Classes). Examples of subject matter not included are: Stereo, sound effects, hearing aids, input and output transducers, and musical instruments.
2. This class includes audio signal processing wherein significant processing is performed to modify the signal's bandwidth or time characteristics for compression or expansion of the signal.

D. COMMUNICATIONS

1. This class does not include subject matter wherein significant details of a distinct communications system or telephone link is performed and speech signal processing is nominally claimed (see Classes 340, 370, 375, 379, 455 in the Search Class notes below in References to Other Classes.).
2. This class includes subject matter directed to speech signal processing disclosed or claimed in plural diverse arts such as various types of communication systems.

E. APPLICATIONS

1. This class does not include subject matter wherein significant details of application systems are performed and speech signal processing is nominally claimed.
2. This class includes subject matter directed to speech signal processing disclosed or claimed in plural diverse arts to include electrical and mechanical systems. Examples would include systems controlled by speech recognition, systems which create specific displays of speech data, systems for editing speech data and otherwise unrelated systems which incorporate speech signal processing details such as placing a speech synthesizer into novelty items.

SEE OR SEARCH THIS CLASS, SUBCLASS:

1 for linguistics.
100 for speech signal processing.
500 for audio compression.

FIGURE 5–11. *(continued)*

REFERENCES TO OTHER CLASSES

SEE OR SEARCH CLASS:

84, Music, 1 for instruments used in producing music to include (a) electrical music instruments, (b) automatic instruments, and (c) hand-played instruments. Automatic and hand-played instruments are divided into four groups: stringed, wind, rigid vibrators, and membranes. This class also includes some accessory devices generally recognized as belonging to the art or industry.

181, Acoustics, various subclasses, for mechanically transmitting, amplifying and ascertaining the direction of sound and for mechanically muffling or filtering sound.

340, Communications: Electrical, 825 for controlling one or more devices to obtain a plurality of results by transmission of a designated one of plural distinctive control signals over a smaller number of communication lines or channels.

341, Coded Data Generation or Conversion, various subclasses for electrical pulse and digit code converters (e.g., systems for originating or emitting a coded set of discrete signals or translating one code into another code wherein the meaning of the data remains the same but the formats may differ).

345, Computer Graphics Processing, Operator Interface Processing, and Selective Visual Display Systems, various subclasses for the selective control of two or more light generating or light controlling display elements in accordance with a received image signal, and 1 for visual display systems with selective electrical control including display memory organization and structure for storing image data and manipulating image data between a display memory and display device.

360, Dynamic Magnetic Information Storage or Retrieval, which is an integral part of Class 369 following subclass 18, for record carriers and systems wherein information is stored and retrieved by interaction with a medium and there is relative motion between a medium and a transducer, for example, magnetic disk drive devices, and control thereof, per se.

365, Static Information Storage and Retrieval, various subclasses for addressable static singular storage elements or plural singular storage elements of the same type (i.e., the internal elements of memory, per se).

• • •

FIGURE 5–11. *(continued)*

200 SPEECH SIGNAL PROCESSING
201 ... For storage or transmission
202 ... Neural network
203 ... Transformation
204 ... Orthogonal functions
205 ... Frequency
206 ... Specialized information
207 ... Pitch
208 ... Voiced or unvoiced
209 ... Formant
210 ... Silence decision
211 ... Time
212 ... Pulse code modulation (PCM)
213 ... Zero crossing
214 ... Voiced or unvoiced
215 ... Silence decision
216 ... Correlation function
217 ... Autocorrelation
218 ... Cross-correlation
219 ... Linear prediction
220 ... Analysis by synthesis
221 ... Pattern matching vocoders
222 ... Vector quantization
223 ... Excitation patterns
224 ... Normalizing
225 ... Gain control
226 ... Noise
227 ... Pretransmission
228 ... Post-transmission
229 ... Adaptive bit allocation
230 ... Quantization
231 ... Recognition
232 ... Neural network
233 ... Detect speech in noise
234 ... Normalizing
235 ... Speech to image
236 ... Specialized equations or comparisons
237 ... Correlation
238 ... Distance
239 ... Similarity
240 ... Probability
241 ... Dynamic time warping
242 ... Viterbi trellis
243 ... Creating patterns for matching
244 ... Update patterns
245 ... Clustering
246 ... Voice recognition
247 ... Preliminary matching
248 ... Endpoint detection
249 ... Subportions
250 ... Specialized models
251 ... Word recognition
252 ... Preliminary matching
253 ... Endpoint detection
254 ... Subportions
255 ... Specialized models
256 ... Markov
257 ... Natural language
258 ... Synthesis
259 ... Neural network
260 ... Image to speech
261 ... Vocal tract model
262 ... Linear prediction
263 ... Correlation
264 ... Excitation
265 ... Interpolation
266 ... Specialized model
267 ... Time element
268 ... Frequency element
269 ... Transformation
270 ... Application
271 ... Handicap aid
272 ... Novelty item
273 ... Security system
274 ... Warning/alarm system
275 ... Speech controlled system
276 ... Pattern display
277 ... Translation
278 ... Sound editing

FIGURE 5–12. SUBCLASSES 200 THROUGH 278.

1. ARTIFICIAL INTELLIGENCE
2. ... Speech signal processing

• • •

2.4 ... Recognition
2.41 ... Neural networks
2.42 ... Detect speech in noise
2.43 ... Normalizing
2.44 ... Speech to image
2.45 ... Specialized equations or comparisons
2.46 ... Correlation
2.47 ... Distance
2.48 ... Similarity
2.49 ... Probability
2.50 ... Dynamic time warping
2.51 ... Viterbi trellis
2.52 ... Creating patterns for matching
2.53 ... Update patterns
2.54 ... Clustering
2.55 ... Voice recognition
2.56 ... Preliminary matching
2.57 ... Endpoint detection
2.58 ... Subportions
2.59 ... Specialized models
2.60 ... Word recognition
2.61 ... Preliminary matching
2.62 ... Endpoint detection
2.63 ... Subportions
2.64 ... Specialized models
2.65 ... Markov
2.66 ... Natural language
2.67 ... Synthesis

• • •

Note: For a complete listing of Class 395 as it appeared when these subclasses were still in use, see Appendix B in the main volume of *Software Patents*.

FIGURE 5–13. 395 CLASS LISTINGS.

Thus, whereas class 395 was once held the primary ground where software patent art was classified, now the 700 series has taken its place. Just as class 395 (Information Processing) had once edged out older class 364 (Electrical Computers) to claim the software limelight, today the 700 series has moved class 395 to the shadows. To paraphrase General Douglas MacArthur, Old classes never die; they just fade away.

With the above history in mind, it is understandable why the examiner included class 395 in the field of search. One might wonder why the examiner's search did not also include the original grandparent class 364. The reason may be one of simple practicality. In January 2001, class 364 contained only three speech recognition patents, and all were of recent vintage and primarily classified elsewhere (in classes 704 and 705). The examiner may have checked this and thus knew that class 364 was not worth searching.

As an interesting point of history, had the examiner attempted to search class 364 for this concept, in say 1980, that search would have been next to impossible. In 1980 an invention in speech processing, like other software inventions, would likely have been classified under the "miscellaneous" subclasses 600 and 900. These were formidably large subclasses that few mortals would ever consider searching by hand. Eventually patent examiners were given rudimentary software tools to aid in searching these subclasses, but those tools had little of the power found in today's full text searching tools.

From the above assessment, we can see that subclasses 242 and 256 seem fairly focused on the problem of speech recognition. The subclass definitions, reproduced in § 5.10[D][4] show these subclasses to be quite specific to certain technical aspects of speech recognition. While worth searching, these subclasses are perhaps somewhat off the mark. In this example we are searching for automated systems that translate spoken broadcast news programs into text summaries. Fortunately, there is a subclass, subclass 277, that deals specifically with translation. It is the child of the "application" parent subclass 270. The search notes (see Fig. 5–11) explain the purpose of this application, grouping such things as:

> . . . subject matter directed to speech signal processing disclosed or claimed in plural diverse arts to include electrical and mechanical systems. Examples would include systems controlled by speech recognition, systems which create specific displays of speech data. . . .

Indeed, a quick keyword search of the term "broadcast" within subclass 277 yields promising results. One of the patents identified is 5,615,310 to Rivers, entitled "Automated Language Translation System," which describes the following translation system:

> A language translation system receives audio output from a television, a radio, or some other electronic device designed to present a program to a user, so as to identify any speech signal contained within the audio output. The speech signals are broken down into recognizable phonemes which make up the most basic elements of speech in spoken languages. The sequentially generated phonemes identified from the speech signals are then regrouped so as to form recognizable words in one of a predetermined number of recognizable languages. Sentences are then formed using the grammatical rules of the recognized language so that each sentence may be translated into a universal language, such as Esperanto. The translation system then translates the sentences from Esperanto to the native language of the user as identified by the user.[57]

Although the 5,615,310 Rivers patent may not specifically describe generating a text summary, it is sufficiently relevant to warrant searching subclass 277.

---

[57] 5,615,310 to Rivers, entitled "Automated Language Translation System," issued March 25, 1997.

In the preceding example, the recommended searching methodology has been illustrated. To aid in conducting other software patent searches using this methodology, § 5.10[E] below presents a detailed taxonomy of the software patent art collection of the U.S. Patent Office, showing how the current subclasses grew from the older computer class roots. Keep in mind that the patent classification system is continually changing. Therefore, periodically check the current Manual of Classification on the Patent Office web site to get the latest revisions.

[E] A Taxonomy of the U.S. Patent Office Software Prior Art Collection

Whether you use a narrow definition of the term "software" or an expansive one, software patent prior art can be found classified in many different places. Most of the newly issuing software patents are classified in the 700 series of the U.S. classification system. However, if you consult the search notes to those classes, you will find there are many other places to look for software patents.

Figure 5–14 gives an overview of the current taxonomy of the software patent prior art. To illustrate how the prior art collection has migrated, Figure 5–15 shows where the software art resided in 1994, when the first edition of this book was written. A lot changed between 1994 and 2001. In 1994, class 395 was the primary class where software patent art was classified. In 2001, the 700 series, comprising eight separate data processing classes, all but replaced class 395. The expansion of the software patent prior art collection from a single class to multiple classes over this seven year period substantiates the unprecedented growth of software patents over that period.

[1] Tracing the Software Patent Roots

It is interesting to trace the roots of that software patent growth. When one does so, one learns that software patents existed long before 1994. Indeed, they have existed for as long as there have been computers, and perhaps even before. Delving into the prior art, one can find early software patents that issued only a few short years after the digital computer was first invented. For example, in May of 1951, Bell Labs was awarded a patent on an "Error-Detecting and Correcting System,"[58] which was a software patent by anyone's definition. But software patent roots extend far earlier than this. In the 1840s Samuel Morse was awarded his famous telegraph patent, in which he included specific claims to his way of encoding information using a series of dots, dashes, and spaces. It is interesting that this claim survived the Supreme Court's scrutiny, whereas Morse's other claims did not. See § 11.02[A] in main volume.

[58] U.S. patent 2,552,629, issued May 15, 1951.

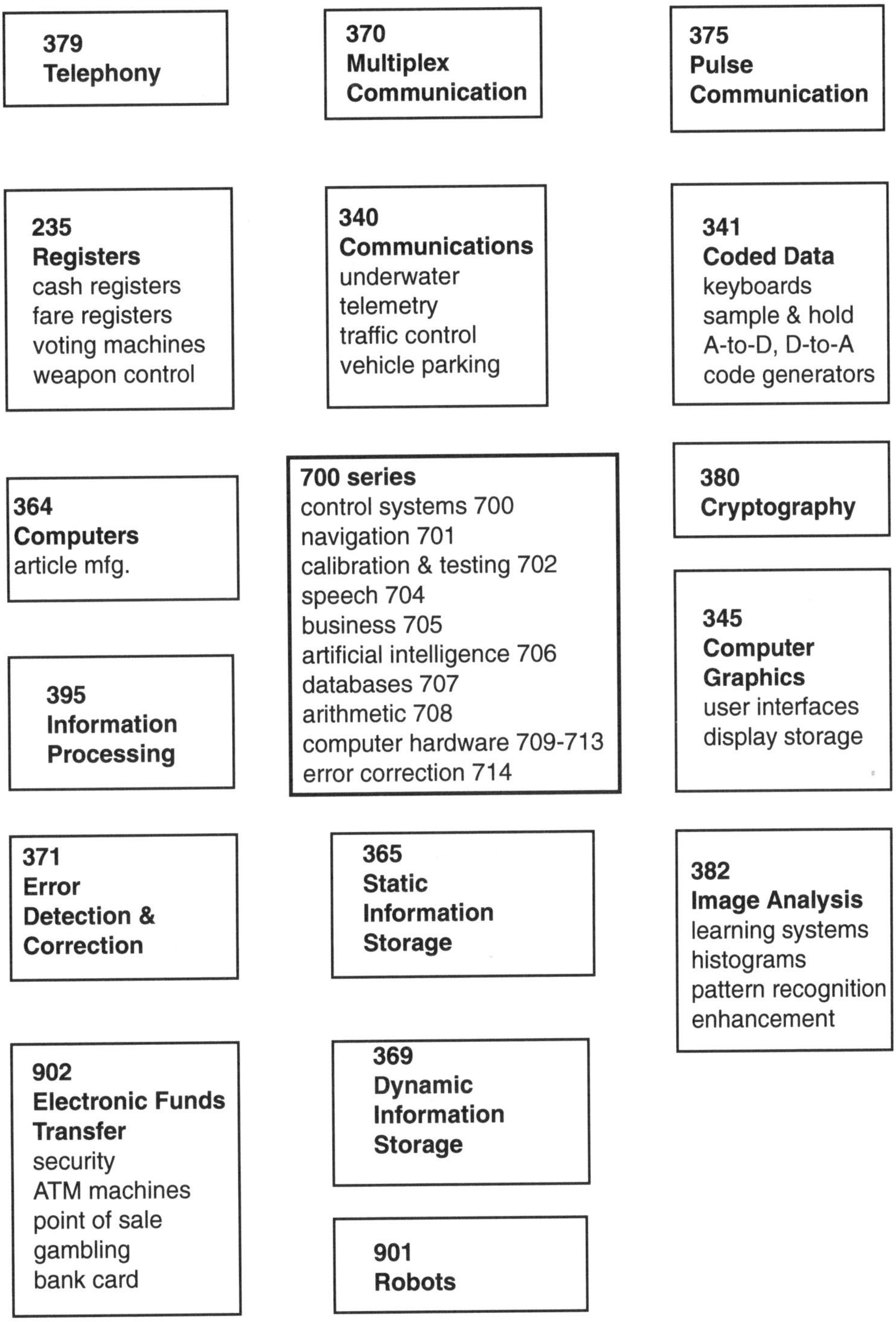

FIGURE 5–14. SOFTWARE PATENT CLASSIFICATION TAXONOMY (2001).

379
Telephony

370
Multiplex
Communication

375
Pulse
Communication

235
Registers
cash registers
fare registers
voting machines
weapon control

340
Communications
underwater
telemetry
traffic control
vehicle parking

341
Coded Data
keyboards
sample & hold
A-to-D, D-to-A
code generators

364
Computers
article mfg.
communications
data collection
education
image processing
language transl.
machine control
medical
music
military

395
Information
Processing
artificial intelligence
speech
robot control
computer graphics
networking
simulation
storage
reliability

380
Cryptography

345
Computer
Graphics
user interfaces
display storage

371
Error
Detection &
Correction

365
Static
Information
Storage

382
Image Analysis
learning systems
histograms
pattern recognition
enhancement

902
Electronic Funds
Transfer
security
ATM machines
point of sale
gambling
bank card

369
Dynamic
Information
Storage

901
Robots

FIGURE 5–15. SOFTWARE PATENT CLASSIFICATION TAXONOMY (1994).

Morse's information encoding claim read as follows:

> I claim, as my invention, the system of signs, consisting of dots and spaces, and of dots, spaces, and horizontal lines, for numerals, letters, words or sentences, substantially as herein set forth and illustrated, for telegraphic purposes.[59]

Whether Morse's claim is entitled to the software patent moniker or not, there are countless software patents and pre-software patents buried within the strata of the massive prior art collection that is the United States Patent Office.

Morse's claim aside, perhaps the software revolution began with the adding machine. That remarkable device of the 1800s finds itself classified in a class now titled, Registers — class 235. It is interesting, however, that class 235 began with a more simple purpose, to classify things with springs. The earliest patent in class 235 was patent number 551 for a Carriage Spring issued to Morton on January 9, 1838. During that era, class 235 also included such diverse items as a Molasses Faucet and a Cooking Stove. Presumably the common element in these devices was a spring that made it work.

However, the dawn of the software age would soon peek out over the horizon. In 1839, the Patent Office issued U.S. patent number 1,325 for an Odometer. It was classified under "Registers." Later, adding machines would adopt the odometer-style readout for showing the sum of numbers being added. Shortly thereafter, in 1843, the Patent Office granted patent number 2,907 for a Slide Rule. The following year, it issued U.S. patent 3,574 to J. Hatfield for a Machine for Calculating Interest, issued May 6, 1844. The following year it issued U.S. patent 4,632 for a Calculator, to Vanderveer, on July 14, 1846 and U.S. patent 4,902 for a Calculating Machine, to McLelman, on December 22, 1846. The software age was on its way.

The "registers" class 235 continued to grow over the next one hundred years. Today it contains patents on cash registers, voting machines, weapon system computers, pocket calculators, and even bar codes. The electronic digital computer was invented in 1945, see main text § 1.03[A][3]. In 1951, when Bell Labs was issued its patent on an "Error-Detecting and Correcting System,"[60] the Patent Office classified this software invention under Telegraphy — class 178. It also cross-referenced the patent under Registers — class 235 and under Coded Data Generation — class 341.

At first, the Patent Office was not sure what to do with software. For instance in 1972 it issued patent number 3,633,176 to Kaiser Aluminum, for a "Recursive Kopy Program for Remote Input Management System."[61] That patent claimed a

---

[59] O'Reilly v. Morse, 56 U.S. 62, 85, 112 (1854).

[60] U.S. patent 2,552,629, issued May 15, 1951.

[61] U.S. patent 3,663,176, issued January 4, 1972.

method of operating a digital computer in a network. The method claimed a recursive algorithm. The Patent Office classified the invention under "Electrical Communications — class 340." Three years later it issued patent number 3,924,078 to The Post Office, London, England, for an "Apparatus for Displaying an Extreme Value Among a Succession of Digital Values."[62] The claims of that patent recited an algorithmic method for determining and displaying a maximum number. Avoiding a pure algorithm recitation, the claims recited that a pulse code modulated signal was used to encode the value. The patent was classified under Multiplex Communication — class 370.

However, by the 1980s class 364 (Electrical Computers and Data Processing Systems) was beginning to fill to the brim with all sorts of computer-related inventions, including pure software inventions. Exemplary of such patents was patent number 4,486,857 entitled, "Display System for the Suppression and Regeneration of Characters in a Series of Fields in a Stored Record."[63] Although you might not recognize the software nature of the invention by the patent title, claim 21 of that patent is pure software:

> 21. A computer program for operating on a file consisting of a plurality of records where each record consists of n ordered fields, F_i where n is greater than one and wherein each field F_i consists of L_i alphanumeric characters, the program operable on a computer having a display capability for S alphanumeric characters, where S is less than the length of the record, the program comprising:
>
> means for recognizing certain preselected alphanumeric characters in each field Fi;
>
> means for selectively removing the recognized preselected characters in each field F_i so that the length L_i of F_i is reduced to a shortened substring f_i of predetermined length l_i less than L_i and then displaying the reduced length substrings f_i on the computer; and
>
> means for displaying a full-length substring F_i selectively chosen from one of the displayed reduced fields f_i while simultaneously displaying at least one other reduced field f_i or f_n.

At some point, class 364 began to attract all sorts of software inventions, often cloaked in hardware language. Because these software-disguised-as-hardware inventions resisted easy classification, examiners found themselves placing many of them in the "miscellaneous" subclasses 364/600 and 364/900. In short order, these subclasses grew to immense size and could not be readily searched by hand.

Recognizing that it needed to address the burgeoning miscellaneous subclasses of class 364, in 1991 the Patent Office created new class 395. Titled, "Information Processing System Organization," this new class served as the new

---

[62] U.S. patent 3,924,078, issued December 2, 1975.

[63] U.S. patent 4,486,857, issued December 4, 1984.

CLASS	1989	1990	1991	1994	1995	1996	1997	1998	1999	Jan 2001 (PTO web site)
235	Registers	--->	--->	--->	--->	--->	--->	--->	--->	--->
340	Communications, electrical	--->	--->	--->	--->	--->	--->	--->	--->	--->
364	Electrical computers and data processing systems	--->	--->	--->	--->	--->	--->	--->	dropped from on-line index	Data Processing Control Systems, Methods or Apparatus
365	Static information storage and retrieval	--->	--->	--->	--->	--->	--->	--->	--->	--->
369	Dynamic information storage and retrieval	--->	--->	--->	--->	--->	--->	--->	--->	--->
370	Multiplex communications	--->	--->	--->	--->	--->	--->	--->	--->	--->
371	Error detection/correction and fault detection/recovery	--->	--->	--->	--->	--->	--->	--->	dropped in favor of 714	--->
375	Pulse or digital communications	--->	--->	--->	--->	--->	--->	--->	--->	--->
379	Telephonic communications	--->	--->	--->	--->	--->	--->	--->	--->	--->
380	Cryptography	--->	--->	--->	--->	--->	--->	--->	--->	--->
382	Image Analysis	--->	--->	--->	--->	--->	--->	--->	--->	--->
455	Telecommunications	--->	--->	--->	--->	--->	--->			--->
395	did not exist	--->	Information processing system organization	--->	--->	--->	--->	--->	--->	--->
700	did not exist	--->	--->	--->	--->	--->	--->	--->	Data Processing: Generic Control systems or specific applications	--->
701	did not exist	--->	--->	--->	--->	--->	Data Processing: vehicles, navigation and relative location	--->	--->	--->
702	did not exist	--->	--->	--->	--->	--->	--->	Data Processing: Measuring, calibrating or testing	--->	--->

FIGURE 5–16. EVOLUTION OF PATENT CLASSES CONTAINING SOFTWARE INVENTIONS.

CLASS	1989	1990	1991	1994	1995	1996	1997	1998	1999	Jan 2001 (PTO web site)
703	did not exist	--->	--->	--->	--->	--->	--->	--->	--->	Data Processing: structural design, modeling, simulation and emulation
704	did not exist	--->	--->	--->	--->	--->	Data Processing: Speech signal processing, linguistics, language translation and audio compression/decompression	--->	--->	--->
705	did not exist	--->	--->	--->	--->	--->	Data Processing: Financial, business practice, management, or cost/price determination	--->	--->	--->
706	did not exist	--->	--->	--->	--->	--->	--->	Data processing: artificial intelligence	--->	--->
707	did not exist	--->	--->	--->	--->	--->	Data Processing: database and file management, data structures, or document processing	--->	--->	--->
708	did not exist	--->	--->	--->	--->	--->	--->	--->	Electrical Computers: arithmetic processing and calculating	--->
709	did not exist	--->	--->	--->	--->	--->	--->	--->	Electrical Computers and digital processing systems: multiple computer or process coordinating	--->
710	did not exist	--->	--->	--->	--->	--->	--->	--->	Electrical computers and digital data processing systems: input/output	--->

FIGURE 5–16. *(continued)*

CLASS	1989	1990	1991	1994	1995	1996	1997	1998	1999	Jan 2001 (PTO web site)
711	did not exist	--->	--->	--->	--->	--->	--->	--->	Electrical computers and digital data processing systems: Memory	--->
712	did not exist	--->	--->	--->	--->	--->	--->	--->	Electrical computers and digital data processing systems: processing architectures and instruction processing	--->
713	did not exist	--->	--->	--->	--->	--->	--->	--->	Electrical computers and digital data processing systems: Support	--->
714	did not exist	--->	--->	--->	--->	--->	--->	--->	Error detection/correction and fault detection/recovery	--->
716	did not exist	--->	--->	--->	--->	--->	--->	--->	Data Processing: design and analysis of circuit or semiconductor mask	--->
717	did not exist	--->	--->	--->	--->	--->	--->	--->	Data Processing: Software development, installation and management	--->
901	Robots	--->	--->	--->	--->	--->	--->	--->	--->	--->
902	Electronic Funds Transfer	--->	--->	--->	--->	--->	--->	--->	--->	--->

FIGURE 5–16. *(continued)*

holding tank for software inventions until the creation of the 700 class series during 1997 to 1999. Developing and populating the 700 series took several years. First on the scene was class 701 (Data Processing: vehicles, navigation, and relative location), which was established in 1997.

Figure 5–16 shows the developmental history of several software-related classes, including the new 700 series classes.

CHAPTER 8

DRAFTING CLAIMS OF PROPER SCOPE

Page 380, add after end of § 8.06:

§ 8.07 CLAIM DRAFTING IN LIGHT OF *FESTO*

On November 29, 2000, the Federal Circuit Court of Appeals handed down a striking *en banc* ruling that the doctrine of equivalents would no longer be applied to claim elements that had been amended during prosecution, where the amendment narrowed the scope of the claim to address any statutory requirement for a patent. The case was *Festo Corporation v. Shoketsu Kinzoku Kogyo Kabushiki Co., Ltd.*[49] In one fell swoop the Federal Circuit court lopped off a mighty branch of claim interpretation.

At issue in *Festo* were two patents, the Stoll patent and the Carroll patent, each covering certain magnetic rodless cylinders used in linear motors. During prosecution of these patents (which included a reexamination of the Carroll patent), the applicant amended certain elements of the claims. Claim 1 of the Stoll patent and claim 9 of the Carroll patent are reproduced below, with underlining included to show some of the language that was added to these claims.

[A] Stoll Patent Claim 1

Claim 1 included the following language:

> 1. In an arrangement having a hollow cylindrical tube and driving and driven members movable thereon for conveying articles, the improvement comprising
>
> wherein said tube is made of a nonmagnetic material,
>
> wherein said driving member is a piston movably mounted on the inside of said tube, said piston having a piston body and plural axially spaced, first permanent annular magnets encircling said piston body,
>
> said piston further including first means spacing said first permanent magnets in said axial spaced relation, the radially peripheral surface of said magnets being oriented close to the internal wall surface of said tube,
>
> said piston further including <u>plural guide ring means</u> encircling said piston body and slidingly engaging said internal wall and
>
> <u>first sealing rings located axially outside said guide rings</u> for wiping said internal wall as said piston moves along said tube to thereby cause any impurities that may be present in said tube to be pushed along said tube so that said first annular magnets will be free of interference from said impurities,
>
> wherein said driven member includes <u>a cylindrical sleeve made of a magnetizable material</u> and encircles said tube,
>
> said sleeve having plural axially spaced second permanent annular magnets affixed thereto and in magnetically attracting relation to said first permanent annular magnets,

---

[49] 234 F.3d 558 (Fed. Cir. 2000).

and second means spacing said second permanent annular magnets in said axially spaced relation, the radially inner surface of said magnets being oriented close to the external surface of said tube,

said sleeve having end face means with second sealing rings located axially outside said second permanent annular magnets for wiping the external wall surface of said tube as said driven member is moved along said tube in response to a driving movement of said piston to thereby cause any impurities that may be present on said tube to be pushed along said tube so that said second permanent annular magnets will be free of interference from said impurities.

[B] Carroll Patent Claim 9

Claim 9 included the following language:

9. A device for moving articles, which comprises:

a hollow cylinder formed of non-ferrous material and having opposite axial ends;

a piston mounted in the interior of the hollow cylinder and reciprocatingly slidable therein, the piston including a central mounting member disposed axially in the cylinder,

a plurality of cylindrically-shaped permanent magnets mounted on the central mounting member and spaced apart axially from each other, each magnet having a bore formed axially there-through for receiving the central mounting member,

at least one pair of end members mounted on the central mounting member and disposed on opposite axial sides of the plurality of magnets, a pair of cushion members formed of resilient material, the cushion members being situated near opposite axial ends of the central mounting member to help prevent damage to the piston when the piston contacts an axial end of the cylinder,

and <u>a pair of resilient sealing rings situated near opposite axial ends of the central mounting member and engaging the cylinder to effect a fluid-tight seal therewith</u>;

a body mounted on the exterior of the hollow cylinder and reciprocatingly slidable thereon,

the body including a plurality of annularly shaped permanent magnets surrounding the cylinder and spaced apart from each other, the permanent magnets of the piston and body being polarized so as to magnetically couple the body to the piston whereby movement of the piston inside the cylinder causes a corresponding movement of the body outside the cylinder,

the body further including means provided thereon for holding on the body an article to be moved; and

means for controlling the admission of pressure fluid into the cylinder and exhaust fluid from the cylinder for moving the piston in the cylinder,

the attractive forces between the permanent magnets of the piston and the body being such that movement of the piston causes corresponding movement of the body below a predetermined load on the body and such that above said predetermined load movement of the piston does not cause corresponding movement of the body.

[C] The Amendments Made to the Stoll and Carroll Claims

Stoll amended the above claim 1, adding the underlined language in response to the examiner's rejection of the claim under 35 U.S.C. §112, first paragraph. The examiner had found the original claims did not meet the §112 statutory requirements because the "exact method of operation is unclear. Is [the] device a true motor or magnetic clutch?"[50] As originally filed, Stoll's claim recited, in its preamble, that the invention was a "linear motor." Apparently, the examiner questioned the accuracy of this and that was the genesis of the §112, first paragraph rejection.

In Stoll's remarks submitted with the amendment, he perfunctorily stated that "each of the claims now present in this application has been reviewed for compliance with the provisions of Title 35 U.S.C. 112. Accordingly, further consideration of these claims, particularly with respect to the provisions of Title 35 U.S.C. 112, is respectfully solicited."[51]

After considering Stoll's response, the examiner allowed the amended claims, requesting that all references to "linear motors" be deleted from the specification, because this phrase connoted a different device having different operating characteristics than the device now claimed.

Carroll's were rejected on prior art grounds. During reexamination, the examiner cited a certain German prior art reference against Carroll's claim 1. In response, Carroll canceled claim 1 and added claim 9 (reproduced above). Unlike claim 1, claim 9 explicitly recited a "pair of resilient sealing rings. . . ." (see underlined language above). In his remarks submitted with the amendment, Carroll argued that the now-amended claims "more clearly and more specifically" define the "features of the patentee's invention that distinguish over the art of record, including" the German patent cited in the request for reexamination.[52] Carroll further stated that "the particular structure of the inner piston and outer body now specifically set forth in new claim 9 is not taught or suggested by the German patent," particularly noting the recitation of the placement and plurality of magnets for both the piston and outer body and the recitation of resilient materials and cushion materials on the ends of the piston.[53]

The examiner allowed the amended claims, stating that the prior art did not teach or render obvious the combination which includes the plurality of magnets, end members, and cushion members in the claimed relationship.[54]

---

[50] Festo Corporation v. Shoketsu Kinzoku Kogyo Kabushiki Co., Ltd., 234 F.3d 558, 583 (Fed. Cir. 2000).

[51] Id.

[52] Id. at 584.

[53] Id.

[54] Id.

[D] The District Court Proceedings

Festo brought suit against Shoketsu Kinzoku Kogyo Kabushiki (also known as SMC Corporation) on both patents and demanded a jury trial. At trial SMC urged that the accused devices had two notable differences from the structures claimed in the patents. First, the accused devices had only a single resilient two-way sealing ring, located on one end of the pistons. Thus, while the patents disclosed and claimed devices with a pair of sealing rings, the accused devices had only one. Second, the outer portion of the sleeves of the accused devices was made of an aluminum alloy, a material that is not magnetizable. Thus, while the Stoll patent disclosed and claimed a sleeve made of magnetizable material, the accused devices had sleeves that were not made of a magnetizable material.

At first blush, it may seem surprising that Festo could cogently argue that non-magnetizable aluminum was equivalent to a magnetizable material. However, Festo offered expert testimony that the accused sleeve of aluminum encircled the magnets and formed a magnetic circuit in substantially the same way as the sleeve of the patent. Both the sleeve of magnetic material and the aluminum sleeve functioned to reduce magnetic leakage.

Before trial, the trial court granted Festo partial summary judgment, finding infringement of the Carroll patent under the doctrine of equivalents. After trial, the jury returned a verdict that the accused devices did not literally infringe the Stoll and Carroll patents. However, the jury concluded that the differences were insubstantial and thus found infringement under the doctrine of equivalents.

SMC had argued unsuccessfully both during summary judgment and at trial that the Stoll and Carroll patents were not entitled to benefit of the doctrine of equivalents, because the differences between the accused devices and the patented devices were precisely in those elements that had been amended during prosecution. SMC argued that Festo was estopped by its amendments from arguing that the single, double acting sealing ring was equivalent to two separate rings, and that non-magnetizable aluminum was equivalent to a magnetizable material.

Festo countered that the amendments Stoll and Carroll had made to the claims were not made to overcome a prior art rejection, but had simply been made to clarify the language of the claims under 35 U.S.C. §112. Thus, Festo argued, it was not prevented by file wrapper estoppel from applying the doctrine of equivalents to these claim elements. Although Carroll claim 9 had been added to overcome a prior art rejection, it had argued differences in the placement of the sealing rings and made no issue whatsoever of the magnetizable sleeve limitation of claim 9. In response to one of the summary judgment motions, the district court concluded that the reason for the magnetizable sleeve amendment was "a mystery," because it did not appear to be related to any of the examiner's §112 rejections, and it did not appear to distinguish the invention over the prior art. (The prior art reference also employed a magnetizable material.)[55]

[55] Id. at 585.

[E] The Court of Appeals Initially Upholds the Trial Court's Ruling and Jury Verdict

SMC appealed the jury verdict and the adverse summary judgment ruling to the Court of Appeals for the Federal Circuit. Judges Rich, Newman, and Michel heard the appeal; Judge Newman wrote the opinion. The court affirmed the grant of partial summary judgment and upheld the jury verdict. The court specifically rejected SMC's position that prosecution history estoppel was applicable.

[F] SMC Appeals to the Supreme Court and Ultimately Wins Reversal

SMC appealed to the U.S. Supreme Court and the Court granted certiorari. In a decision published March 17, 1997 the Court vacated the prior decision and remanded the Court of Appeals for further consideration in light of *Warner-Jenkinson Co. v. Hilton Davis Chem. Co.,* 520 U.S. 17 (1997).[56] With the case back on its docket, the Federal Circuit Court of Appeals initially denied SMC's suggestion that the case be heard en banc. Ultimately, in an order published August 20, 1999, the Court of Appeals decided to hear the case en banc and asked the parties to address the following five questions in their briefs:

> 1. For the purposes of determining whether an amendment to a claim creates prosecution history estoppel, is "a substantial reason related to patentability," *Warner-Jenkinson Co. v. Hilton Davis Chem. Co.,* 520 U.S. 17, 33, 117 S. Ct. 1040, 137 L. Ed. 2d 146 (1997), limited to those amendments made to overcome prior art under § 102 and § 103, or does "patentability" mean any reason affecting the issuance of a patent?
> 2. Under *Warner-Jenkinson,* should a "voluntary" claim amendment — one not required by the examiner or made in response to a rejection by an examiner for a stated reason—create prosecution history estoppel?
> 3. If a claim amendment creates prosecution history estoppel, under *Warner-Jenkinson* what range of equivalents, if any, is available under the doctrine of equivalents for the claim element so amended?
> 4. When "no explanation [for a claim amendment] is established," *Warner-Jenkinson,* 520 U.S. at 33, 117 S. Ct. 1040, thus invoking the presumption of prosecution history estoppel under *Warner-Jenkinson,* what range of equivalents, if any, is available under the doctrine of equivalents for the claim element so amended?
> 5. Would a judgment of infringement in this case violate *Warner-Jenkinson's* requirement that [*6] the application of the doctrine of equivalents "is not allowed such broad play as to eliminate [an] element in its entirety," 520 U.S. at 29, 117 S. Ct. 1040. In other words, would such a judgment of infringement, post Warner-Jenkinson, violate the "all elements" rule?[57]

[56] Shoketsu Kinzoku Kogyo Kabushiki Co. v. Festo Corp., 520 U.S. 1111, 137 L. Ed. 2d 323, 117 S. Ct. 1240 (1997).

[57] Festo Corp. v. Shoketsu Kinzoku Kogyo Kabushiki Co., 187 F.3d 1381, 1381-82, 51 U.S.P.Q.2d 1959, 1959-60 (Fed. Cir. 1999).

[G] The En Banc Ruling in *Festo*

As to how the court answered the five questions it had posed, the answers were shocking to some. Judge Schall, writing for the majority, summed up the court's answers as follows:

> Question 1
>
> For the purposes of determining whether an amendment to a claim creates prosecution history estoppel, is "a substantial reason related to patentability," *Warner-Jenkinson Co. v. Hilton Davis Chem. Co.,* 520 U.S. 17, 33, 117 S. Ct. 1040, 137 L. Ed. 2d 146 (1997), limited to those amendments made to overcome prior art under § 102 and § 103, or does "patentability" mean any reason affecting the issuance of a patent?
>
> We answer Question 1 as follows: For the purposes of determining whether an amendment gives rise to prosecution history estoppel, a "substantial reason related to patentability" is not limited to overcoming or avoiding prior art, but instead includes any reason which relates to the statutory requirements for a patent. Therefore, a narrowing amendment made for any reason related to the statutory requirements for a patent will give rise to prosecution history estoppel with respect to the amended claim element.
>
> Question 2
>
> Under *Warner-Jenkinson,* should a "voluntary" claim amendment — one not required by the examiner or made in response to a rejection by an examiner for a stated reason — create prosecution history estoppel?
>
> We answer Question 2 as follows: Voluntary claim amendments are treated the same as other amendments. Therefore, a voluntary amendment that narrows the scope of a claim for a reason related to the statutory requirements for a patent will give rise to prosecution history estoppel as to the amended claim element.
>
> Question 3
>
> If a claim amendment creates prosecution history estoppel, under *Warner-Jenkinson* what range of equivalents, if any, is available under the doctrine of equivalents for the claim element so amended?
>
> We answer Question 3 as follows: When a claim amendment creates prosecution history estoppel with regard to a claim element, there is no range of equivalents available for the amended claim element. Application of the doctrine of equivalents to the claim element is completely barred (a "complete bar").
>
> Question 4
>
> When "no explanation [for a claim amendment] is established," *Warner-Jenkinson,* 520 U.S. at 33, 117 S. Ct. 1040, thus invoking the presumption of prosecution history estoppel under *Warner-Jenkinson,* what range of equivalents, if any, is available under the doctrine of equivalents for the claim element so amended?

> We answer Question 4 as follows: When no explanation for a claim amendment is established, no range of equivalents is available for the claim element so amended.
>
> Question 5
>
> Would a judgment of infringement in this case violate *Warner-Jenkinson's* requirement that the application of the doctrine of equivalents "is not allowed such broad play as to eliminate [an] element in its entirety," 520 U.S. at 29, 117 S. Ct. 1040. In other words, would such a judgment of infringement, post *Warner-Jenkinson,* violate the "all elements" rule?
>
> We do not need to reach this question for reasons which will become clear in our discussion of the specific case before us. Accordingly, we leave for another day any discussion of the "all elements" rule.[58]

The majority opinion, written by Judge Schall, was joined to varying degrees by the remainder of the court. Figure 8–2 contains a breakdown of how the judges voted on the five questions set forth above.

As Figure 8–2 shows, a large majority of the court was in general agreement. Question 3 appeared to present the most problem: If there has been a prosecution history estoppel, what range of equivalents is available for the amended element?

[H] Michel's Dissenting Opinion

It concerned Judge Michel that the majority was reducing the range of equivalents to zero for an amended claim element. This, he believed, upset the balance struck by the Supreme Court in *Warner-Jenkinson* between the competing needs for meaningful patent protection and adequate public notice. Judge Michel made his point, with a striking exposition on how a would-be copyist could readily avoid infringement of any patent, simply by substituting an equivalent for an amended claim element.

> Would-be copyists, of course, will exploit the majority's bar. Unwittingly, the majority has severely limited the protection previously available to patentees. Indeed, it may nullify the doctrine of equivalents. Under the majority's approach, anyone who wants to steal a patentee's technology need only review the prosecution history to identify patentability-related amendments, and then make a trivial modification to that part of its product corresponding to an amended claim limitation. All the other limitations may be copied precisely. The competitor will then be free to make, use, or sell an insubstantial variant of the patentee's invention.[59]

---

[58] Festo Corp. v. Shoketsu Kinzoku Kogyo Kabushiki Co., Ltd., 234 F.3d 558, 578 (Fed. Cir. 2000).

[59] Id. at 600-601.

	Question 1	Question 2	Question 3	Question 4	Question 5
Mayer	MAJOR	MAJOR	MAJOR	MAJOR	MAJOR
Newman	*N*	*N*	*N*	MAJOR	MAJOR
Michel	MAJOR	MAJOR	*M; R*	MAJOR	MAJOR
Plager	MAJOR; P	MAJOR; P	MAJOR; P	MAJOR; P	MAJOR; P
Lourie	MAJOR; Lo	MAJOR; Lo	MAJOR; Lo	MAJOR; Lo	MAJOR; Lo
Clevenger	MAJOR	MAJOR	MAJOR	MAJOR	MAJOR
Rader	MAJOR	MAJOR	*R; M; Li*	MAJOR	MAJOR
Schall	MAJOR	MAJOR	MAJOR	MAJOR	MAJOR
Bryson	MAJOR	MAJOR	MAJOR	MAJOR	MAJOR
Gajarsa	MAJOR	MAJOR	MAJOR	MAJOR	MAJOR
Linn	MAJOR	MAJOR	*Li; R*	MAJOR	MAJOR
Dyk	MAJOR	MAJOR	MAJOR	MAJOR	MAJOR

Majority Opinion
by Schall = MAJOR

Concurring Opinions
Plager = P
Lourie = Lo

Dissenting-in part Opinions
Michel = *M*
Rader = *R*
Linn = *Li*
Newman = *N*

FIGURE 8–2. BREAKDOWN OF JUDICIAL VOTES IN *FESTO*.

Judge Michel believed that the court should make some range of equivalents available even to amended elements in the claim. He predicted that patent applicants, now without recourse to the doctrine of equivalents, would likely file many more administrative and judicial appeals rather than acquiesce to patentability rejections. That, he predicted, would further clog the already backlogged docket of the Board of Patent Appeals and Interferences and further lengthen the average time and cost of obtaining a U.S. patent.

[I] Claim Drafting Considerations and Strategies

The court in *Festo* has substantially withdrawn the reach of the doctrine of equivalents. Why is this so? Perhaps it is because a large majority of patent cases today are tried to a jury, and the court has grown weary of countermanding aberrant jury verdicts where the doctrine of equivalents has run amok. Perhaps the court is trying to trim back the power of the jury, shifting even more power to the trial judge, whose duty it is to construe the claims and instruct the jury on their meaning. Regardless of the reason, *Festo* provides a clear signal that the court intends to continue the linguistic manner in which claims are interpreted today.

Prior to the formation of the Court of Appeals for the Federal Circuit in 1982, patent appeals were heard by the federal appellate court within the jurisdiction where the trial was held. Bench trials were far more popular than jury trials. These trials tended to focus more on whether the accused had appropriated the "invention," with far less attention paid to any hypercritical reading of the words of the patent claims. It is understandable why this was so. With the trial judge construing the claims and assessing the issue of infringement, strict claim construction rules were probably not required.

However, with the advent of the Federal Circuit Court of Appeals, and the overall unification and strengthening of the patent system, jury trials have grown increasingly popular. Claim construction is now of paramount importance. No longer is the trial judge permitted to review the patent claims to determine the "essence" of the invention. Now the claim language must be carefully scrutinized in light of the patent specification and prosecution history. Every word counts. This hyper-focus on the claims has turned the patent trial into a linguistic contest, in which each side now twists and pulls at every word of the claim, that it might ensnare the accused device, or set it free.

So, what is to be done with *Festo?* On the defensive side, companies fearful of being drawn into unwarranted patent infringement litigation can breath a sigh of relief. So long as literal infringement has been avoided, *Festo* provides a powerful lever with which to pry the lid off a would-be plaintiff's case. Archimedes is said to have held the Roman navy at bay during the siege of Syracuse using a long and powerful lever with which he actually lifted the attacking ships by the prow high into the air and then dropped them, causing them to fill with water and capsize.[60] In the right hands *Festo* becomes a similar lever. Judge Michel's dissenting opinion contains the blueprint for such a lever. Identify claim language that was amended and replace the amended elements with equivalent structure that does not literally infringe.

From the patent applicant's side, *Festo* creates a big problem, and the available countermeasures are expensive, with no guarantees. The problem with *Festo* from the patent applicant's standpoint is quite evident. The applicant is not prescient. The applicant does not know *in advance* how the examiner is going to rule on the submitted claims, and there is little opportunity to find out. Before *Festo* a common claiming strategy dictated that the applicant should submit claims seeking somewhat broader coverage than the applicant expected to get. Those claims would be rejected in the first office action, and the examiner's rejection of those claims would give the applicant knowledge about where to focus the claims for his or her next attempt. The initially submitted claims, and the first office action by the examiner was akin to dipping one's toe in the hot tub before jumping in.

Now, after *Festo,* one can no longer test the patent waters without risk of inadvertently creating an estoppel condition. While *Festo* has given the public

[60] Polybius, The Rise of the Roman Empire (Penguin: 1980).

better notice of what subject matter to avoid, *Festo* has taken away one of the patent applicant's tools for finding out what not to claim in the first place.

What countermeasures are available to the patent applicant? They fall into three categories: (1) get as much information as possible about the prior art and about the examination process before submitting the claims, (2) submit claims in various formats and of varying scope and (3) do not routinely acquiesce when the examiner characterizes claim language objections in statutory terms. These countermeasures are no crystal ball, but they can help strengthen the patentee's position in two respects. First, resulting patents have more claims, of varying perspective and scope, increasing the chances that literal infringement may be found. Second, estoppel is minimized by increasing the chances that at least some claims will be allowed without requiring amendment. The following sub-sections explore these countermeasures in greater detail.

[1] *Festo* Countermeasure One: Obtaining Information About the Prior Art and About the Examination Process

When the Software Patent Institute (SPI) was formed to develop a body of software prior art, its board of directors initially assumed that the Institute could fund itself from prior art searching fees charged to users of the system. The SPI board was disappointed to learn that most large corporate software developers — which, in addition to the Patent Office, were expected to be the biggest users of the SPI database — did not routinely conduct pre-filing prior art searches. These companies did conduct extensive art searches when sued for patent infringement, of course. But fortunately for them, and unfortunately for SPI, patent infringement lawsuits were comparatively rare.

The rationale behind *not searching* for prior art went like this. Our inventors generally know the state of the art because they practice in the field daily and regularly attend symposia and seminars in their field. Art searches give us little additional information and are therefore a waste of money. Moreover, if we do conduct a search, and learn of a pertinent patent in the process, our knowledge of that patent will be held against us if we are ever sued for infringement of that patent. In short, if the patent did not turn up during our patent clearance due diligence search, conducted prior to product launch, we don't want to know about it. Finally, the Patent Office is going to conduct a search anyway. Why not let them do their job.

Festo has tarnished this *not searching* strategy. If a company wants to obtain effective patents, it can no longer adopt the head-in-the-sand policy of filing applications blind. To minimize the risk of a *Festo* estoppel, applicants need better knowledge — not about the prior art, per se — but about what the patent examiner is likely to cite against the submitted claims. In other words, even the most knowledgeable research scientist or engineer profits by conducting a prior art search because that search may reveal art he or she will have to address during prosecution. It may not even be the closest prior art; but if the examiner cites it, the applicant has no choice but to respond.

It is of course possible to conduct a pre-filing prior art search. Many applicants have done this for years, despite the current popularity of the *not searching* strategy. If the search is a good one, it can help immeasurably when drafting the initial set of claims. However, a good prior art search is no panacea. The examiner may cite other art, and often does. Indeed, some examiners will cite and apply art they have uncovered even if the best art was supplied by the applicant. Perhaps this is just human nature. The examiner's bible, the Manual of Patent Examining Procedure, dictates that the examiner shall conduct a search. Thus the examiner will search and is likely to find something. After having gone to the trouble of finding a piece of prior art, the examiner then feels obliged to cite it.

Not all art cited during patent prosecution is actually *applied* in rejecting the claims. Some art is merely cited as being of general background interest. The examiner selects which art to apply in supporting a rejection under 35 U.S.C. §§ 102 and 103. Thus, during prosecution, the art cited as background interest are soldiers standing at the sidelines of the battlefield, warning the applicant not to direct the course of prosecution in their direction. The art applied by the examiner are the soldiers the examiner has placed on the battlefield and whom the applicant must defeat in order to win a patent.

Experienced examiners know to apply the closest, most pertinent art, even if the applicant initially cited it to the examiner. However, inexperienced examiners will sometimes overlook the closest art and instead apply the art found in the examiner's search. This difference between experienced and inexperienced examiners makes the claim drafter's job very difficult. In drafting an initial set of claims to avoid statutory rejections over the known closest art, one cannot readily account for an ill-chosen reference by the inexperienced examiner. That is not to say that all inexperienced examiners do this. Most are well supervised. But it does happen. The problem is compounded by the high employment turnover rate at the Patent Office.

While prior art searches can be of assistance in anticipating rejections under 35 U.S.C. § 102 and § 103, currently there is no effective way to predict what other statutory rejections may be raised. True, one can carefully draft the initial set of claims to avoid any blatant 35 U.S.C. § 112 problems. However, some examiners will use the § 112 rejection as a preface to every non-art issue they wish to raise, even if the issue is not truly a statutory one. For example, some examiners will purport to apply 35 U.S.C. § 112, second paragraph, merely to have the applicant correct the spelling of a misspelled word. While bad spelling may be a sin, it hardly seems to rise to a statutory level. The statute requires particularity and distinctiveness; it doesn't require correct spelling:

> The specification shall conclude with one or more claims particularly pointing out and distinctly claiming the subject matter which the applicant regards as his invention.[61]

[61] 35 U.S.C. § 112, second paragraph.

Can anything be done to stave off such non-prior art statutory rejections? Using a spell checker would be the obvious place to start. But the problem covers far more territory than merely bad spelling. What you need is the best possible knowledge of the examination process. That entails knowing not only the statutory and regulatory procedures, but also knowing the examining corps. Know the rules and know who you are dealing with. An ideal place to start in learning the rules, is the Manual of Patent Examining Procedure (MPEP). While the MPEP is merely a restatement of the rules — a secondary authority, not a primary one — it does reflect how the examiners are trained to apply the rules.

Collecting information on who you are dealing with, that is, on the examiners themselves, takes ingenuity. While there is nothing like personal experience, it is the rare patent attorney who knows the examiners in a particular art unit before drafting the initial set of claims. *Festo* has squelched one's opportunity to use the examination process to get to know the examiner directly. Now one must use indirect, and admittedly less effective, investigative techniques.

To gain an understanding of the examining corps who will be examining the claims of your application, begin by identifying what art unit the application will be assigned to. This can be done by looking at related patents in the field, uncovered during prior art searching. From these patents, identify who the examiners are, noting in particular who the Primary Examiners are. If you plan to prosecute several applications in a given art unit, it may be worthwhile to get to know the Primary Examiner(s) in that art unit and related art units before preparing the applications.

Much of the responsibility of training new examiners falls on the Primary Examiners. Thus these Primary Examiners are naturally interested in ways to improve the quality of the examinations performed under their supervision. Certainly the fewer § 112 issues their new examiners encounter, the more time they will have to concentrate on the prior art. In this context, many Primary Examiners are quite happy to discuss with you the kinds of § 112 issues they most frequently encounter. They can shed valuable light on how you can avoid such issues in the first place. In this regard, keep in mind that the new examiners often learn to spot § 112 issues based on what their Primary Examiner or supervisor has taught them to look for. Knowing *what* issues examiners are looking for can greatly help you draft the application to avoid those issues.

[2] *Festo* Countermeasure Two: Submit Claims of Varying Scope and Perspective

The equivalents-damaging effect of *Festo* begins when the examiner rejects the initially submitted claims for any statutory basis. This includes rejections for:

- lack of novelty under 35 U.S.C. § 102,
- obviousness under 35 U.S.C. § 103,
- lack of patentable subject matter under 35 U.S.C. § 101,

- failure to provide information in the specification sufficient to enable one to practice the invention under 35 U.S.C. § 112, first paragraph,
- failure to describe in the specification the best mode contemplated by the inventor of carrying out the invention 35 U.S.C. § 112, first paragraph,
- failure to provide a written description of the invention under 35 U.S.C. § 112, first paragraph,
- failure to particularly point out and distinctly claim the invention under 35 U.S.C. § 112, second paragraph, and
- claiming an inoperative invention which fails to satisfy the utility requirement under 35 U.S.C. § 101.

Thus, to avoid the effects of *Festo,* one can try to avoid getting a statutory rejection in the first place. That is far more easily said than done. The Manual of Patent Examining Procedure, which dictates how the examiners conduct examination and prepare office actions, is replete with examples showing examiners how to make statutory rejections. It is a rare patent that is allowed without at least one statutory rejection in its file history. Nevertheless, if the effects of *Festo* are to be abated, there are claiming strategies one can adopt to increase the chances of having at least *some* initially submitted claims allowed without statutory rejection. This said, it is still unreasonable to expect *all* initially submitted claims to be allowed without statutory rejection. To achieve this result, one would likely need to file only claims of narrow scope that avoid the prior art by a wide margin. Such strategy risks giving up patent coverage the applicant would otherwise be entitled to claim. The better strategy involves a carefully crafted range of claims, of varying scope and perspective.

Claiming an invention is like painting a three dimensional object on a two dimensional canvas. The outcome depends on the painter's vantage point and perspective. One can view an invention from far above, rendering general features and broad details; or one can move in close and render specific features in great detail. In figurative terms, the invention may look like one thing when viewed from the front, and another thing when viewed from the side or rear. Thus, when claiming an invention it makes sense to think about vantage point. Find the best vantage points and draft claims directed to each.

[a] Claim Vantage Points Based on Statutory Subject Matter

How can you identify the best vantage points? One way is to think about the different kinds of subject matter that are eligible for patent protection. The patent statute provides that

> Whoever invents or discovers any new and useful process, machine, manufacture, or composition of matter, or any new and useful improvement thereof,

> may obtain a patent therefor, subject to the conditions and requirements of this title.[62]

Thus, you can think about an invention in general terms as a (1) process or method, (2) machine or apparatus, (3) article of manufacture, (4) composition of matter, or (5) improvements. Within each of these general categories lie numerous subcategories.

For example, many software inventions will involve some new way of organizing data — a new data structure. Although the new data structure itself is an abstraction, in a working implementation, the data is likely to be stored in a computer-readable memory and the new data structure dictates how the data is organized and stored in that memory. Thus in linguistic terms the data structure is no longer an abstraction but rather an adjective, describing how the computer memory is configured. In the statutory context, computer-readable memory is an "article of manufacture" with the data structure describing the details about what is new about this manufacture.

From a slightly different viewpoint, the same data structure may also be used to dictate how data is organized while being delivered over a communication medium, such as over a network. Under the Patent Office guidelines governing software inventions, a data structure embodied in a carrier wave also constitutes an article of manufacture. Section 14.14 of the main text of *Software Patents* describes this interesting variation on the article of manufacture theme.

From yet another vantage point, the data structure may also be a component within a larger software system. The software system can be claimed as a machine or apparatus, with the data structure embodied in some form of data store comprising one of the elements of the machine or apparatus.

Additionally, the data structure may also be recited in the context of a process or method. There are several techniques that can be used to recite a data structure in a method claim. Because the data structure, *per se,* is considered an abstraction, it can be added to a method step in a variety of ways. Method steps often begin with a gerund (a noun formed from a verb by adding *-ing*) to describe an action or process step. Data structures can thus be included in method steps as illustrated by the following examples: "providing a data structure . . ." or "storing a data structure . . ." or "operating upon a data structure . . ."

[b] Claim Vantage Points Based on Inventive Feature

Using the subject matter categories to organize your thinking is one good way to help see the invention from different vantage points. Another good way is to identify the features and advantages of the invention and to draft claims to those features and advantages. Claiming features may seem self-evident. However, often one can get bogged down in the technological aspects of an invention and simply

---

[62] 35 U.S.C. § 101.

overlook all the possibilities. One systematic way to avoid this is to develop a feature matrix. Begin by listing all of the features and advantages in a vertical column of a spreadsheet or grid. Then list all of the different contexts or uses of the invention in a horizontal row along the top of the spreadsheet or grid. These columns and rows thus define the inventive space occupied by the invention. The space is bounded in the vertical dimension by its different points of novelty and in the horizontal dimension by its different aspects of utility.

Once the axes of the grid have been defined, consider each cell within the grid, noting to which column and row each cell belongs. Then for each cell, consider how to claim the feature assigned to that cell's row in the context of the use assigned to that cell's column. Do not expect every cell to demand a different claim strategy. Often features and uses are sufficiently related to warrant a similar claiming treatment.

To illustrate, consider the following example. The invention is a personal finance management system employing software agents that handle the drudgery of paying bills, managing banking records, preparing tax returns, and minding the budget. Unlike prior art systems, which are computer platform-specific and must be run on a standalone computer, the invention is platform-independent and can be run from any Internet-connected computer that happens to be available to the user. This is made possible by a distributed data storage architecture, coupled with innovative security measures. The user configures the software agents to automatically interact with the electronic commerce systems of the mortgage company, the gas company, the electric company, the phone company, and so forth. The software agent not only pays bills but also examines the bills to verify that nothing is awry. Thus, if the electric company erroneously debits the user's account with the electric charges for the nearby aluminum processing plant, the agent detects this and notifies the user before paying the bill.

The invention is currently targeted to the home user as a personal finance manager. However, the inventor envisions other markets, including the small business market. In this market the invention would be incorporated into a bookkeeping and accounting system. In addition, the agent technology may be adapted for use in solving more specific tasks, such as examining cellular telephone bills for fraud. Moreover, while the system is currently designed to be configured and controlled by the end user (the bill payer), the technology can also be incorporated as a feature offered by service providers, including banks, mortgage companies, and utility companies.

The matrix for this invention might look something like that shown in Figure 8–3. The matrix helps you think about how to direct claims to each feature, in the specific context of the field of use specified. To illustrate, consider the first listed feature: platform independent. Software developers strive for platform-independence because it means they only have to develop one product that will serve multiple platform markets. While that is indeed a desirable goal, the software-independent aspect of the invention may impact customers in entirely different ways than the developers were thinking.

	Home User	Small Business	Usage Fraud Detection Applications	Operated by Vendor	Banks	Mortgage Companies	Utility Companies
Platform-Independent							
Internet-Based							
Can Use from any Computer							
Data Storage Is Distributed							
Data Storage Is Secure							
Uses Software Agents							
Software Agents Automatically Interact with Vendor Systems							
Software Agents Audit Bills for Discrepancies							

FIGURE 8–3. EXAMPLE MATRIX TO ANALYZE WHAT TO CLAIM.

For example, to the home user, platform independence means the user can access his or her banking records from state-of-the-art workstation at the office and also from an outdated personal computer at home. The home user does not buy the product because it was easier for the software developer to design. But the home user will buy the product if it offers the greater convenience of being able to work in multiple locations. Similarly, to the small business user, platform independence may allow computers in different departments, running different operating systems, to interact with the bookkeeping and accounting records of the company. In this case, the platform independent feature represents different selling points in these two markets. The matrix helps you identify and direct claims to these differences.

Thus, for the home user market, you might focus a claim on the benefit that the user can bank at home or bank at work — without the need to lug around laptop computers or engage in the ritual of transporting backup copies to and from work. For the small business market, you might focus a claim on integrating departments that use otherwise incompatible equipment.

To further illustrate with another example, consider how the software agents will automatically audit bills for discrepancies. Here the home user may value this as a time saving feature. Using the software agents to screen incoming bills, the user can automate bill paying to a high degree, without fear that an automatic deduction system will go awry and deplete the user's account. To the small business, the same software agents may represent an anti-embezzlement feature. The software agents could expose unusual expenditures and thereby allow the employer to investigate and curtail acts of embezzlement before they got out of hand. To a utility provider or service provider, such as a cable television provider, the software agents could detect abnormal usage patterns, allowing the provider to notify its customer as a courtesy.

That courtesy could include notifying a parent by phone or e-mail concurrently as an x-rated program is being ordered. In a highly competitive market, such a feature could be the determining factor upon which the subscription decision is made.

In each case described above, the feature (software agent detecting abnormal usage) impacts different markets in very different ways. Once you discover these differences it becomes much easier to construct claims to cover the possibilities. The matrix gives you a systematic way to think through the possibilities when meeting with the inventor or management of the inventor's company.

The matrix can also be used as a final cross-check, to make sure nothing has been overlooked. After drafting your initial set of claims, test them against the matrix. Consider how each claim would play in an infringement action where a party identified in one of the columns is competing with the patentee in a market where the feature identified in one of the rows is key to making the sale. With that context in mind, ask yourself whether your claims reasonably protect the invention, given the state of the art in which the invention arose. Doing this for each cell in the matrix may help you discover holes in your claim drafting strategy. While your strategy may not fully block all of the *Festo* holes, it will give the patentee far more options for enforcing the patent using a literal infringement analysis, thereby avoiding *Festo* altogether.

[3] *Festo* Countermeasure Three: Do Not Acquiesce to Inappropriate Statutory Rejections

Under pre-*Festo* practice, applicants would regularly acquiesce to rejections under 35 U.S.C. § 112, because it was easier, quicker, and less expensive to simply correct the wording of a claim rather than argue with the examiner over it. No longer. Now, under *Festo,* a § 112 rejection is a statutory rejection and acquiescence is doomed to a later equivalence reading of the amended language. Thus, as a countermeasure against *Festo,* applicants now may need to dispute far more § 112 and § 101 rejections than ever before.

However, this third countermeasure should be handled delicately. Examiners are not always tuned in to how their office actions may impact subsequent litigation involving the patents they issue. This is particularly true when it comes to the doctrine of equivalents, because the doctrine is applied when the act of alleged infringement occurred, not when the patent was examined and issued. In the words of the Supreme Court:

> Insofar as the question under the doctrine is whether an accused element is equivalent to a claimed element, the proper time for evaluating equivalency — and knowledge of interchangeability between elements — is at the time of infringement, not at the time the patent was issued.[63]

Under a doctrine of equivalents analysis, a court or jury may be asked to consider, as equivalent, certain technology that arose after the application was examined and the patent was issued.

> . . . an equivalent under the doctrine of equivalents may arise after patent issuance and before the time of infringement. *See Warner-Jenkinson.* An "after-arising" technology could thus infringe under the doctrine of equivalents without infringing literally as a § 112, paragraph 6 equivalent.[64]

Because examiners are not able to assess the equivalence of such after-developed technology, it is quite understandable that examiners are not taught to concern themselves with the doctrine of equivalents issue.

The net effect is that some examiners may not be sensitive to *Festo*-borne problems arising from the purported statutory rejections that they make. The following subsections address various nonprior art statutory rejections and explain when and how to argue around them.

[a] Failure to Particularly Point Out and Distinctly Claim

The patent statute at 35 U.S.C. § 112, second paragraph, sets forth the requirement that the applicant for a patent must submit claims "particularly pointing out and distinctly claiming the subject matter which the applicant regards as his invention." This requirement may form the basis for all manner of rejections where the examiner does not find the submitted claim language to be suitable. Whether

[63] Warner-Jenkinson Co. v. Hilton Davis Co., 520 U.S. 17 (1997).

[64] Al-Site Corp. v. VSI Intern., Inc., 174 F.3d 1308, 1320 (Fed. Cir. 1999).

the examiner's reasons for rejecting the claim language rises to a statutory level is the issue to be determined. The Manual of Patent Examining Procedure describes the purpose of § 112, second paragraph, as twofold:

> The primary purpose of this requirement of definiteness of claim language is to ensure that the scope of the claims is clear so the public is informed of the boundaries of what constitutes infringement of the patent. A secondary purpose is to provide a clear measure of what applicants regard as the invention so that it can be determined whether the claimed invention meets all the criteria for patentability and whether the specification meets the criteria of 35 U.S.C. 112, first paragraph with respect to the claimed invention.[65]

Thus, the claim language needs to be sufficient to (a) inform the public and (b) allow the examiner to search for prior art and assess whether the specification meets the written description, enablement, and best mode requirements.

This statutory requirement places the public's shoes on the examiner's feet. The examiner has the responsibility to ensure that the public receives notice of the full metes and bounds of the patent grant, and acquires full knowledge of the applicant's invention or discovery. The statutory requirement does not give the examiner carte blanche power to require changes in the claim language merely because the examiner would prefer it. 35 U.S.C. § 112, second paragraph, establishes an objective standard, not a subjective one. The Manual of Patent Examining Procedure contains support for this.

In explaining 35 U.S.C. § 112, second paragraph, the Manual notes that there are two requirements set forth in this statutory paragraph:

> (A) the claims must set forth the subject matter that applicants regard as their invention; and
>
> (B) the claims must particularly point out and distinctly define the metes and bounds of the subject matter that will be protected by the patent grant.[66]

The Manual goes on to explain that while the first requirement is subjective, the "particularly pointing out and distinctly claiming" requirement is objective.

> The first requirement is a subjective one because it is dependent on what the applicants for a patent regard as their invention. The second requirement is an **objective** one because it is not dependent on the views of applicant or any particular individual, but is evaluated in the context of whether the claim is definite — i.e., whether the scope of the claim is **clear to a hypothetical person possessing the ordinary level of skill** in the pertinent art. (emphasis added)[67]

[65] Manual of Patent Examining Procedure § 2173.
[66] Manual of Patent Examining Procedure § 2171.
[67] Manual of Patent Examining Procedure § 2171.

Because 35 U.S.C. § 112, second paragraph, embodies two requirements, a subjective one and an objective one, the Manual instructs the examiner to make clear in the office action whether a 35 U.S.C. § 112, second paragraph rejection is directed to the first requirement or the second:

> If a rejection is based on 35 U.S.C. 112, second paragraph, the examiner should further explain whether the rejection is based on indefiniteness or on the failure to claim what applicants regard as their invention. *Ex parte Ionescu,* 222 U.S.P.Q. 537, 539 (Bd. App. 1984).[68]

If the rejection is based on the subjective reason — that the claim is not directed to what the applicants regard as the invention — this can be addressed by showing that the specification does support the subject matter claimed, because the claims are considered part of the specification, as discussed in the next subsection. On the other hand, if the rejection is based on the objective reason, that the claims are indefinite, then your response may seek to show that the claim language would be clear to one of ordinary skill in the art.

Here is where it gets sticky. Patent applicants are permitted to be their own lexicographers. Patent examiners are instructed to recognize this and to interpose their lexicographical judgment only where the claim language would not be clear to one of ordinary skill in the art. However, when confronted with a statutory rejection under 35 U.S.C. § 112, second paragraph, the examiner has probably already made up his or her mind that the objected to claim language is not clear. How do you convince the examiner to withdraw the rejection? One place to begin is with the Manual of Patent Examining Procedure. The Manual provides a good basis for arguing that a wide latitude is permitted under the patent laws:

> A fundamental principle contained in 35 U.S.C. 112, second paragraph is that applicants are their own lexicographers. They can define in the claims what they regard as their invention essentially in whatever terms they choose so long as the terms are not used in ways that are contrary to accepted meanings in the art. Applicant may use functional language, alternative expressions, negative limitations, or any style of expression or format of claim which makes clear the boundaries of the subject matter for which protection is sought. As noted by the Court in *In re Swinehart,* 439 F.2d 210, 160 U.S.P.Q. 226 (C.C.P.A. 1971), a claim may not be rejected solely because of the type of language used to define the subject matter for which patent protection is sought.[69]

Note the wide latitude the above passage permits. The applicant may use:

- functional language
- alternative expressions

---

[68] Manual of Patent Examining Procedure § 2171.

[69] Manual of Patent Examining Procedure § 2173.01.

- negative limitations
- *any* style of expression
- *any* format of claim

so long as the result makes clear the boundaries of the subject matter for which protection is sought. The Manual explains that the examiner is merely to examine the claim language to ensure it meets a certain threshold of clarity and precision. While the examiner is encouraged to make suggestions in claim language, where appropriate, those suggestions need not be accompanied by a statutory rejection under 35 U.S.C. § 112, second paragraph.

> The examiner's focus during examination of claims for compliance with the requirement for definiteness of 35 U.S.C. 112, second paragraph is whether the claim meets the threshold requirements of clarity and precision, not whether more suitable language or modes of expression are available. When the examiner is satisfied that patentable subject matter is disclosed, and it is apparent to the examiner that the claims are directed to such patentable subject matter, he or she should allow claims which define the patentable subject matter with a <u>reasonable</u> degree of particularity and distinctness. Some latitude in the manner of expression and the aptness of terms should be permitted even though the claim language is not as precise as the examiner might desire. Examiners are encouraged **to suggest claim language to applicants to improve the clarity or precision of the language used,** but should not reject claims or insist on their own preferences if other modes of expression selected by applicants satisfy the statutory requirement. (underlining in original, bold emphasis added)[70]

Thus, when faced with a rejection under 35 U.S.C. § 112, second paragraph, one might want to discuss the section of the Manual excerpted above with the examiner. See if the examiner can be persuaded to withdraw the rejection and instead characterize his or her observations as a suggestion to improve clarity or precision. If the examiner wishes to engage in a rigorous analysis as to whether the rejection under 35 U.S.C. § 112, second paragraph, is proper, be prepared to address the following points stated in the Manual.

> The essential inquiry pertaining to this requirement is whether the claims set out and circumscribe a particular subject matter with a reasonable degree of clarity and particularity. Definiteness of claim language must be analyzed, not in a vacuum, but in light of:
> (A) The content of the particular application disclosure;
> (B) The teachings of the prior art; and
> (C) The claim interpretation that would be given by one possessing the ordinary level of skill in the pertinent art at the time the invention was made.

[70] Manual of Patent Examining Procedure § 2173.02.

> If the scope of the invention sought to be patented cannot be determined from the language of the claims with a reasonable degree of certainty, a rejection of the claims under 35 U.S.C. 112, second paragraph is appropriate. *In re Wiggins,* 488 F.2d 538, 179 U.S.P.Q. 421 (C.C.P.A. 1973).[71]

In preparing to address these points, note whether similar language has been used in the prior art. If the objected to language is found in the prior art, you are in a good position to argue that the language would be understood to persons of ordinary skill in the art and thus meets the objective standard for definiteness.

In the *Wiggins* case, cited as authority by the Manual, the state of the prior art cut against the applicant's position. Wiggins's invention was for a chemical formulation claimed to have efficacy in treating Parkinson's disease. His claim recited only part of the chemical formulation, a heterocyclic group, leaving the remainder of the formulation open ended. The examiner and the Board of Appeals felt that the term "heterocyclic group" was not precise enough to allow the scope of the claims to be accurately determined. Wiggins had disclosed a heterocyclic group containing a carbon atom — which Wiggins asserted had therapeutic properties. However, within the prior art there were other heterocyclic groups containing other atoms. There was no evidence these other prior art formulations had the claimed therapeutic properties, hence the scope of the invention was unclear from the claim language.

[b] Failure to Recite What Applicant Regards as the Invention

You really should not get a 35 U.S.C. § 112, second paragraph rejection on this basis in the first office action. If you do, chances are good you can have the rejection retracted. The Manual of Patent Examining Procedure is clear that a rejection on this basis is only made where the applicant has stated, in some document other than the patent application itself, that the invention is different from what is defined in the claims. In other words, the invention set forth in the claims is presumed, in absence of evidence to the contrary, to be that which the applicant regards as the invention.[72] Applicant's specification cannot be used as evidence that the scope of the claims is inconsistent with the subject matter regarded as the invention.[73]

Of course, if the application has a history of prior admissions made in briefs or remarks then a rejection on this basis may be proper. Therefore use care when characterizing the invention in arguments made in briefs and remarks accompanying amendments.

Sometimes an examiner will note that the language of the claims does not match the description in the specification. This can happen when the claims and

[71] Manual of Patent Examining Procedure § 2173.02.

[72] Manual of Patent Examining Procedure § 2172 I.

[73] Manual of Patent Examining Procedure § 2172 II.

specification are drafted separately and the language chosen in one has not been conformed to the language chosen in the other. Although it is incorrect to do so, some examiners will seize upon this language nonconformity as grounds for rejecting the claims under 35 U.S.C. § 112, second paragraph. The basis of the rejection is that the claims fail to recite what the applicant regards as his or her invention. This basis is fallacious. The claims submitted with the application form part of the specification. Thus it is improper to reject those claims as not having basis in the specification.

If you get a rejection under 35 U.S.C. § 112, second paragraph, based on a failure to recite what applicant regards as the invention, you can launch your response from the Manual of Patent Examining Procedure. The Manual explains that this rejection is improper, and that the proper rejection should be directed to the specification using 35 U.S.C. § 112, first paragraph.

> The content of applicant's specification is not used as evidence that the scope of the claims is inconsistent with the subject matter which applicants regard as their invention. As noted in *In re Ehrreich,* 590 F.2d 902, 200 U.S.P.Q. 504 (C.C.P.A. 1979), agreement, or lack thereof, between the claims and the specification is properly considered only with respect to 35 U.S.C. 112, first paragraph; it is irrelevant to compliance with the second paragraph of that section.[74]

At first blush, it would seem that using the above argument is merely trading one statutory rejection for another. However, from the *Festo* standpoint this may not be altogether bad. If the examiner's true objection is that the language of the claims and the language of the specification do not match, it should be possible to amend the *specification* to match the language of the claims. This would arguably not be adding any new matter, because the specification includes the claims as filed. Hence the matter being added to the specification is not new to the application. More importantly, by amending the specification you avoid making amendments to the claims which might trigger *Festo* consequences.

Of course, a rejection under 35 U.S.C. § 112, first paragraph (e.g., failure to meet written description, enablement, or best mode requirements) may still have estoppel consequences. The majority opinion in *Festo* specifically listed § 112, first paragraph, rejections among those statutory rejections that might be applied in rejecting the claims. Thus it is conceivable that a court might view a corrective amendment to the specification as creating estoppel even though the claims were not amended. Care should be used in drafting any accompanying remarks to such a corrective amendment. Make it clear that the corrective amendment is being done simply to conform or unify the language throughout the application and without changing what the applicant regards as his or her invention.

---

[74] Manual of Patent Examining Procedure § 2172 II.

§ 8.08 HOW COURTS CONSTRUE THE CLAIMS YOU DRAFT

People who grew up with English as their mother tongue have enjoyed its rich, expressive power and have learned to ignore its shortcomings when it is not always precise. Many English-speaking people tend to believe that their language is somehow superior when it comes to expressing scientific or business ideas. Actually, according to language scholars, English is no better or worse than any other language. According to language scholar David Crystal, any perceived superiority of one language over another is largely myth:

> Latin and Greek were for centuries viewed as models of excellence in western Europe because of the literature and thought which these languages expressed; and the study of modern languages is still influenced by the practices of generations of classical linguistic scholars. . . .
>
> A Linguistic Myth — A belief that some languages are intrinsically superior to others is widespread, but it has no basis in linguistic fact. Some languages are of course more useful or prestigious than others, at a given period of history, but this is due to the preeminence of the speakers at that time, and not to any inherent linguistic characteristics. . . . Perhaps one day some kind of objective linguistic evaluation measure will be devised; but until then, the thesis that some languages are intrinsically better than others has to be denied.[75]

Perhaps the reason there is no evidence of a "superior" language is that language itself is very strongly tied to thought. In that regard, certainly no one culture has an innate superiority over any other. There is, however, an interesting hypothesis, developed by the American linguist and anthropologist, Edward Sapir (1884-1939) and his student Benjamin Lee Whorf (1897-1941) that language actually determines how we think. If not actually in control, language nevertheless influences how we perceive and remember. As a consequence of this, individual languages end up encoding the cultural differences between people. The principle is called *linguistic relativity.* Here is how Whorf explains it:

> We dissect nature along lines laid down by our native languages. The categories and types that we isolate from the world of phenomena we do not find there because they stare every observer in the face; on the contrary, the world is presented in a kaleidoscopic flux of impressions which has to be organized by our minds — and this means largely by the linguistic systems in our minds. We cut nature up, organize it into concepts, and ascribe significances as we do, largely because we are parties to an agreement to organize it in this way — an agreement that holds throughout our speech community and is codified in the patterns of our language. The agreement is, of course, an implicit and unstated

---

[75] David Crystal, The Cambridge Encyclopedia of Language 7 (1987).

> one, *but its terms are absolutely obligatory;* we cannot talk at all except by subscribing to the organization and classification of data which the agreement decrees.[76]

Linguistic relativity manifests itself in a panoply of interesting differences between vocabularies among different cultures. The Eskimo people (who live in snow) have a multitude of different words for snow; the Aztec people (who probably saw little snow) used a single word (with different endings) to cover a whole range of cold, icy, and snowy experiences.

[A] The Nature of Patent Claims

Considering how intimately language is tied to ideas and thought, one can better appreciate the metaphysical purpose behind the patent claim: to project the inventor's ideas into the judicial mind. In the United States district courts judges speak English. Hence the patent judicial system is strongly biased to that language.

The United States patent laws are quite clear about the bias towards English. Indeed, even international applications filed with the U.S. Patent Office must be in English: "International applications filed in the Patent and Trademark Office shall be in the English language."[77] While it is permitted to initially file a patent application in another language, eventually that application must be submitted in English.[78] That includes the claims, which must accompany every regular application: "The specification shall conclude with one or more claims particularly pointing out and distinctly claiming the subject matter which the applicant regards as his invention."[79]

The claims of the application become one of the principal points of focus during prosecution of the application by the patent examiner. After allowance of the application it is again the claims that become the principal focus should the patent ever be employed in an infringement action. It goes without saying that the claims, which are drafted in English, prosecuted in English, and construed in English, inherit all of the strengths and weaknesses of the English language.

Claim drafting is no easy task. Patent practitioners understand this all too well. In drafting claims, the practitioner must learn the subtleties of the invention or discovery, distill from that invention or discovery what the inventor believes is the inventive concept, and then express that inventive concept in a single English sentence called a claim. Although there is no limit to the number of claims an applicant can submit — within reason — each claim stands alone as a single English sentence expression of an inventive concept.

---

[76] *Id.* at 15.
[77] 35 U.S.C. § 361(c).
[78] 35 U.S.C. § 365(c).
[79] 35 U.S.C. § 112, para 2.

This can be quite a heavy burden for a single English sentence to bear. Many English words have different meanings, ranging from subtle to profound. Despite the admonishment of 35 U.S.C. § 112, that the applicant shall "... particularly point out and distinctly claim the subject matter that he regards as his invention," the inherent imprecision of English is always present. Does a simple two-letter word, like "or" (as in A or B) include or exclude the concept of A and B? You would think such a question should be easy to answer, but it is not. Consider these two sentences:

I plan to sign up for mathematics or history next term.

If the forecast calls for snow or sleet, the schools will be closed.

In the above example, perhaps most will agree that the first sentence takes an "exclusive or" construction. Given the propensities of most students not to overtax their studious faculties, we know that the author of the first sentence does not plan to take both mathematics *and* history in the same term. If extrinsic evidence is permitted to be considered, it may turn out that both courses are offered at the same time, thus making it impermissible to sign up for both.

The second sentence certainly takes a different, "inclusive or" construction. There is little doubt that little Johnnie's parents are not going to bundle him up for school if the forecast calls for snow *and* sleet.

So there it is. At a quite fundamental level, English can be very imprecise. Is there a remedy? Patent attorneys are often heard to espouse that the applicant be his or her own lexicographer. In other words, the applicant can make up new words, or give nonstandard meanings to existing words. While this rule gives the claim drafter a lot of freedom, such freedom may not always be a good thing. Given the heavy burden each single sentence claim must carry, playing around with the ordinary meaning of words may simply confuse things, or at least give your claim construction opponent fodder to confuse things.

The Federal Circuit Court of Appeals, if given the opportunity, has every right to construe your claims anew, even if the district court has already done this. Whereas the district court has had the opportunity to meet the inventor, view the invention, study the accused device, and hear the facts firsthand, the court of appeals is constrained to a study of the written record. This places a natural emphasis on *writings* about the invention, rather than on the invention itself. It also creates a framework for review in which all appellate judges have great expertise — construing writings in the English language. Although patent law is a law of invention and discovery, appellate judges are not required to have science or technical degrees. Thus, claim construction often transforms the scientific or technical inquiry into a linguistic puzzle.

The next few sections will explore some linguistic puzzles that have arisen during claim construction in actual cases. The examples have been selected to show how even the simplest words can become the focal point during judicial review.

[B] When "Or" Means "And," and When It Does Not

There are few words simpler than the word "or." Yet this seemingly simple, two-letter staple of the English language can get the unwitting patent applicant into a lot of trouble. A case in point is *Kustom Signals, Inc. v. Applied Concepts, Inc.,*[80] a case of patent claim construction before the Federal Circuit Court of Appeals that turned precisely on the meaning of "or."

The patent-in-suit involved a technology that many motorists are all too familiar with: the traffic radar. Among the often used excuses proffered in traffic courts throughout the country is this one:

> Your honor, it was not I that was speeding. That semi truck coming up fast in my rearview mirror must have swamped the officer's radar. I was only doing forty-five.

In fact, early traffic radar did occasionally have trouble separating two signals, and this could work to the speeder's benefit. Quite commonly, a slower target with a stronger signal (the large truck) would obscure a faster target with a weaker signal (the speeding red Corvette). That problem has largely been solved today through digital signal processing.

U.S. patent 5,528,246,[81] the patent-in-suit owned by Kustom Signals, Inc., described a traffic radar that employed digital signal processing to discriminate between targets based on both size and speed. Using a mathematical technique known as Fast Fourier Transform (FFT), the patented traffic radar would analyze the reflected radar signal's frequency (indicating target speed) and amplitude (indicating target size). Although the device had the ability to analyze either frequency or amplitude, the radar operator manually selected which analytic technique to use, by selecting either the "fastest signal" search mode or the "strongest signal" search mode.

The accused device used similar signal processing techniques, except that both a "fastest signal" analysis and a "strongest signal" analysis were always performed. The radar operator could then select one of three different displays: (1) fastest signal only, (2) strongest signal only, or (3) both fastest and strongest signals simultaneously. Thus, whereas Kustom's preferred embodiment placed the operating mode selection prior to the signal processing step, the accused Applied Concepts placed operating mode selection after the signal processing step. See Figure 8–4.

Although different because of when the operator's manual selection was utilized, the Applied Concepts radar was clearly capable of providing the same kind of information to the user, using essentially the same digital signal processing techniques. Whether the Applied Concepts device infringed Kustom's claims turned out to hinge on the interpretation of a single word, "or."

---

[80] Kustom Signals, Inc. v. Applied Concepts, Inc., 264 F.3d 1326 (Fed. Cir. 2001).

[81] U.S. patent No. 5,528,246 (issued June 19, 1996).

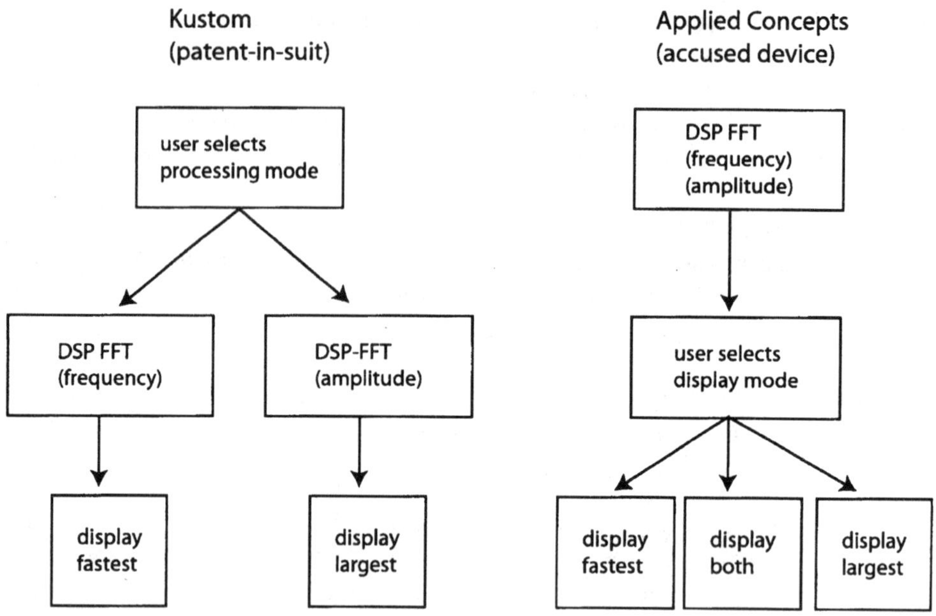

FIGURE 8–4.

[1] Kustom's Method Claim

Kustom's patent contained both method and apparatus claims. The method claim is reproduced below, with emphasis added to the ill-fated word, "or." Note that the claim states that the processing mode (magnitude or frequency) is *predetermined* (e.g., by the operator).

> 1. A method of processing Doppler return information in a traffic radar comprising the steps of:
>
> [a] receiving Doppler return information containing at least one return signal derived from a target vehicle,
>
> [b] presenting said Doppler return information as digital data,
>
> [c] transforming said data into the frequency domain to provide a spectrum that includes frequency components corresponding to Doppler return signals contained in said information,
>
> [d] storing said components in a memory,
>
> [e] searching said components in memory for the component that meets preselected magnitude ***or*** frequency criteria, and
>
> [f] indicating the speed of the target vehicle corresponding to the component that meets said criteria.

In attempting to apply its claim to the Applied Concepts device, Kustom argued that the accused device met every limitation. With respect to paragraph [e] of the claim, Kustom analyzed it this way. Does the accused device search components in memory for components that meet preselected magnitude criteria? Yes. Does the accused device search components in memory for components that meet preselected frequency criteria? Yes. Thus, the accused device literally meets all aspects of the claim limitation.

The problem was, as Applied Concepts pointed out, the accused device did not selectively search its memory for one component *or* the other. The accused device always searched *both*. Thus, Applied Concepts argued its device did not perform the "or" part of the claim limitation. The parties found themselves locked in a dispute whether "or" should have an inclusive meaning (as Kustom argued) or an exclusive meaning (as Applied Concepts argued). Digital circuit designers have long understood the difference between these two interpretations. To be clear about which meaning is intended, circuit designers use the designation OR to convey the inclusive meaning and XOR to convey the exclusive meaning.

[2] The Prosecution History Guides the Federal Circuit to Rule that "Or" Excludes "And"

Kustom had a pretty good argument that "or" should be given an inclusive meaning. It cited the Microsoft Press Computer Dictionary, which distinguishes (as a digital circuit designer would) among logical operators. Microsoft Press thus discriminates among "or" (which returns a "true" value when one or both values are true), "and" (which returns a "true" value if and only if both values are true), and "exclusive or" (which returns a "true" value when only one value is true). Kustom cited precedent that cautioned against construing technical terms of the art at issue in accordance with nontechnical dictionary definitions, instead of the technical usage of the field of the invention.

Unfortunately for Kustom, it had a problem with its argument that stemmed from the patent prosecution history. This prosecution history played a critical role in the court's decision. With a different prosecution history, Kustom's argument might have won. Here is what transpired during prosecution.

Originally, Kustom presented a claim that did not include clauses 1[d], 1[e], and 1[f]. Instead, it recited a spectrum validation process and the step of "determining the magnitude and frequency." During prosecution Kustom added clauses 1[d], 1[e], and 1[f] and described its invention to the examiner as having "multi-mode operation," whereby the desired mode, whether magnitude (strongest target) or frequency (fastest target) would be selected by the operator. The court seized on this as an admission that the exclusive or definition was intended:

> It is apparent that the modes of search and display were intended, in the '246 invention, to be selected in the alternative. The prosecution history requires that "or" means the operator's choice between search for the strongest or fastest target speed, but not both.[82]

[82] Kustom Signals, Inc. v. Applied Concepts, Inc., 264 F.3d 1326, 1331 (Fed. Cir. 2001).

[3] Doctrine of Equivalents Cannot Save the Day for Kustom

Software engineers will perceive a few differences between the Kustom and Applied Concepts approaches. Whether these are technologically substantial or insubstantial depends on the capabilities of the digital signal processing technology. In the Kustom approach, only one type of FFT analysis must be performed (frequency or amplitude). In the Applied Concepts approach, both types of FFT analysis are always performed (frequency and amplitude). If the FFT algorithms are computationally expensive, such that performing both frequency and amplitude requires significantly more computation time, or significantly more powerful processors, then there is a good argument why Kustom's approach and Applied Concepts' approach are substantially different.

On the other hand, if available processing power renders any speed difference or processing requirements moot, then one can appreciate why Kustom believed the differences between the two approaches were insubstantial. Indeed, Kustom submitted testimony that to change its A or B approach into an A and B approach involved the mere addition of a simple programming link. The problem with Kustom's argument was that, in the eyes of the court, Kustom had given up the "and/or" subject matter during prosecution. In the words of the district court, which the Federal Circuit Court of Appeals ratified:

> Plaintiff could have foreseen the alteration of the patented invention from "or" to "and." Indeed, plaintiff claims that it intended to patent a fastest feature that would display the fasted target "either in lieu of the strongest target vehicle or in addition to the strongest vehicle's speed. . . . Despite plaintiff's apparent attempt to draft an "and/or" claim, plaintiff must accept the limited "or" claim it obtained from the PTO. '[A]s between the patentee who had a clear opportunity to negotiate broader claims but did not do so, and the public at large, it is the patentee who must bear the cost of its failure to seek protection for this foreseeable alteration of its claimed structure.' *Sage Products v. Devon Industries,* 126 F.3d 1420, 1425 (Fed. Cir. 1997).[83]

[4] The Dissent

Judge Mayer saw things differently, and his dissent shows how even agreeing on the ordinary meaning of a word like "or" can be difficult. The majority said it was adopting the ordinary meaning when it defined A or B to exclude A and B. Judge Mayer's dissent cogently arrived at a different ordinary meaning:

> In this case, "or" should be construed inclusively to mean "one or another or both." First, the plain meaning of "or" can be "either or both." If a store owner

[83] Kustom Signals, Inc. v. Applied Concepts, Inc., 52 F. Supp. 2d 1260, 1282 (D.Kan. 1999).

says, "If it hails or snows today, we will close the store," then the owner will still close the store if it happens to hail and snow.[84]

Judge Mayer made an even more fundamental observation, however. In referring to the patent specification, Judge Mayer observed that the patented system actually did "search" both the strongest and fastest signals. In so noting, Judge Mayer peels back another layer of this claim-construction onion. Perhaps the dispute should not be with the meaning of "or" but with the meaning of exactly what processes must be carried out to determine if the magnitude and frequency components meet a *preselected criteria.*

> Regardless of whether the operator selects the fastest or strongest mode, both the strongest and the fastest signals are always "searched" (as the district court construed the term). The signals are saved in the indexed array, and duplicated, with one set sorted by decreasing magnitude (finding the "strongest" signal) and the other sorted by decreasing frequency (finding the "fastest" signal).[85]

As for the prosecution estoppel perceived by the majority, Judge Mayer did not find any.

[5] Be Cautious of Powerful Words Like "Or"

Hindsight is 20-20, they say. Yet when wielding powerful words like "or," the odds of being right are 50-50 — even if you have hindsight on your side. Because the court construed "or" to exclude "and" in this case, does not mean it will be construed "or" the same way in patent claims you draft. "Or" has two, bi-stable states. Sometimes the tree falls in your yard, and sometimes it falls on your roof. You have to take particular care (in drafting the specification and in prosecuting the claims) to ensure that your tree will always fall where you want it to.

Of course, "or" is not the only word to be cautious of. There are dozens of others. Be cautious of words that create an absolute condition, such as "always," "never," "only," "all," "prevent," "eliminate," and "not." These are powerful words that can confine your claim to a less expansive interpretation.

When it comes to "or," there are several alternate approaches you may want to try in order to avoid an unwanted construction. One is the classic Markush claiming phraseology favored by chemical practitioners:

> selected from the group consisting of A, B and combinations thereof.

---

[84] Kustom Signals, Inc. v. Applied Concepts, Inc., 264 F.3d 1326, 1333 (Fed. Cir. 2001).

[85] Kustom Signals, Inc. v. Applied Concepts, Inc., 264 F.3d 1326, 1334 (Fed. Cir. 2001).

Using that type of phraseology in Kustom's claim, the language might look like this:

> 1. A method of processing Doppler return information in a traffic radar comprising the steps of:
>
> [a] receiving Doppler return information containing at least one return signal derived from a target vehicle,
>
> [b] presenting said Doppler return information as digital data,
>
> [c] transforming said data into the frequency domain to provide a spectrum that includes frequency components corresponding to Doppler return signals contained in said information,
>
> [d] storing said components in a memory,
>
> [e] searching said components in memory for the component that meets **criteria selected from the group consisting of preselected magnitude criteria, preselected frequency criteria and combinations thereof,** and
>
> [f] indicating the speed of the target vehicle corresponding to the component that meets said criteria.

If that phraseology seems too stilted or unnatural for your particular invention, try replacing "or" with "at least one of . . ."

> at least one of A and B

If we use the latter suggestion in Kustom's claim, the operative language might look like this:

> 1. A method of processing Doppler return information in a traffic radar comprising the steps of:
>
> [a] receiving Doppler return information containing at least one return signal derived from a target vehicle,
>
> [b] presenting said Doppler return information as digital data,
>
> [c] transforming said data into the frequency domain to provide a spectrum that includes frequency components corresponding to Doppler return signals contained in said information,
>
> [d] storing said components in a memory,
>
> [e] searching said components in memory for the component that meets **at least one of the following criteria: (1)** preselected magnitude **criteria and (2) preselected** frequency criteria, and
>
> [f] indicating the speed of the target vehicle corresponding to the component that meets said criteria.

The astute reader may point out that the above claim may not distinguish over the prior art (depending on the state of that art). For example, what if the prior art only operates on the magnitude criteria (and always ignores the frequency criteria). Then one might arguably be able to read the above claim on the prior art, assuming all other limitations [a]–d] and [f] are met. If you confront that situation, consider refining the language a bit to clarify that a selection among choices is meant. For example:

> [e] searching said components in memory for the component that **selectively** meets at least one of the following criteria: (1) preselected magnitude criteria and (2) preselected frequency criteria

Yet another approach to consider is to simply recite, A or B or both. That is, in effect, how dissenting Judge Mayer read the Kustom claims anyway. Doing so would make it clear that the "inclusive or" definition was intended by the applicant. The operative language in Kustom's claim might have looked like this:

> [e] searching said components in memory for the component that meets preselected magnitude or frequency criteria **or both,**

Absent any prosecution history estoppel or language in the specification to the contrary, such a change to the claim would probably suffice to encompass the Applied Concepts device. On the other hand, it would seem to leave open the possibility that a device performing A or B, but *never both* (the exclusive OR behavior), might slip through the claim's grasp.

[C] When "After" Includes "Before" (and When It Does Not)

Having mastered Boolean logic (expressions like "or" and "and"), it is time to move on to temporal logic (expressions like "before" and "after"). Surprisingly, there may be unseen temporal gremlins lurking in these simple English words, as well.

The patent owner in *Oak Technology, Inc. v. International Trade Commission*[86] became painfully aware of this as its claim for compact disk drive controller software underwent scrutiny first by the U.S. International Trade Commission and then by the Federal Circuit Court of Appeals. Under the judicial microscope in that case was the simple temporal-evoking term "after."

Oak Technology owned U.S. patent 5,581,715[87] on certain technology used to detect and correct errors in compact disk drives. It had initiated proceedings before the International Trade Commission, invoking § 337 of the Tariff Act of 1930,[88] seeking to prevent several parties (MediaTek, Inc., United Microelectronics Corporation, Lite-On Technology Corporation, and AOpen, Inc.) from importing certain accused CD-ROM controllers into the United States. The International Trade Commission ruled that the accused controllers did not infringe Oak Technology's patent. Oak Technology appealed to the Federal Circuit Court of Appeals.

---

[86] Oak Technology, Inc. v. International Trade Commission, 248 F.3d 1316 (Fed. Cir. 2001).

[87] U.S. patent No. 5,581,715 (issued December 3, 1996).

[88] 19 U.S.C. § 1337(a)(1)(B).

[1] How Errors Are Detected and Fixed in Compact Disks

To understand the claim construction issue the Federal Circuit faced, it is helpful to understand a little about how error detection and error correction are performed in compact disks. Compact disks, whether they store music, computer program code, or other digital data, have one technological problem in common. Smudges, scratches, dirt, and fingerprints seemingly can't resist taking up residence on the shiny, information-bearing side of the disk. When they do, the laser beam sometimes has trouble seeing through the haze and ends up mistaking zeros for ones and ones for zeros. Sometimes these tiny digital mistakes cause imperceptible distortion — a fleck of color within the rose turns brown or Dolly's sonorous voice for an instant turns dull. Other times these digital mistakes cause more profound results — the disk won't play, or worse, it does play, but with critical errors: The 10.5 pound thrust value is misread as 105 pounds, causing the spacecraft's Martian orbit to decay in a meteoric burst.

When you consider that a typical compact disk stores millions of these ones and zeros, it is truly astounding that they work at all. Fortunately, early compact disk developers worked out a system for detecting and correcting all but the most pernicious reading errors. Adopted as something called the Yellow Book standard, the developers proposed a couple of digital tricks to detect and repair errors. They proposed to detect errors using a well-known scheme, the cyclic redundancy check (CRC). To repair errors detected, they proposed using a different technique known as the Reed-Solomon algorithm.

The CRC is an error-detection scheme that uses special error detection bits, called parity bits, that are generated from the original digital data and then appended to the original digital data. A special polynomial calculation generates the parity bits so that each uniquely corresponds to the original data from which it was generated. Thereafter, if either the original digital data or the parity bits are somehow mangled by being misread, the unique correspondence between the two is lost, and this serves as a signal that an error has occurred.

The Reed-Solomon algorithm serves the different purpose of fixing errors. While that might seem like magic, it really is not. The Reed-Solomon error-correction algorithm, like any error-correction algorithm, relies on redundancy. In a simple, brute-force error-correction scheme one might simply store multiple copies of the data in different places on the disk. That way if one copy is found to contain errors, you fix them by referring to one or more of the other copies. The Reed-Solomon algorithm is considerably more sophisticated than this. Instead of redundantly storing multiple copies in brute-force fashion, the Reed-Solomon algorithm hides redundancy information within specially designed polynomial relationships computed using the original data being safeguarded.

Conceptually, the Reed-Solomon code specifies a polynomial by "plotting" a large number of points into a curve that is then specified by polynomial coefficients. For example, say the original data plots out as a parabola-shaped curve. Mathematicians know that a parabola-shaped curve (or any other smooth and continuous curve) can be described by a polynomial equation ($y=a_0+a_1x+a_2x^2+\ldots a_nx^n$) where the coefficients $a_0,a_1,\ldots a_n$ are numerically specified. The polynomial, once constructed and stored, can then serve to correct any errant bits that no longer lie on the curve as they once did. Just as it is easy for the eye to spot and correct a few bad points that do not lie on the curve, so too can the Reed-Solomon code spot and correct bad data points that no longer fall within the polynomial.

[2] Oak Technology Versus the Competition

The dispute between Oak Technology and MediaTek, et al., turned on the order in which the MediaTek device performed error detection and error correction. Oak Technology's patent claims could be read to suggest one order, whereas MediaTek's device arguably performed these functions in a different order. Oak Technology maintained that its claims were broad enough to cover MediaTek; MediaTek and the International Trade Commission saw things differently.

[a] Oak Technology's Claims

Claim 1 of Oak Technology's patent reads as follows:

> 1. A compact disk drive controller to control the communication of data between a compact disk in a compact disk drive and a host computer via an IDE/ATA data bus, said data bus for receiving and transmitting data between said controller and said host computer, said disk drive having drive electronics that include a digital signal processor and a microcontroller, said controller comprising:
>
> a digital signal processor interface for receiving data from said digital signal processor, said digital signal processor interface descrambling and assembling data received from said digital signal processor;
>
> memory means for temporarily storing data, said memory means temporarily storing said assembled data;
>
> data error detection and correction means for correcting said assembled data, said detection and correction means including error correction circuitry for performing error correction on said assembled data and a cyclic redundancy checker for detecting errors in said assembled data after correction of said data by said correction circuitry for providing corrected data; and
>
> host interface means for connecting said host computer to said controller, said interface means adapted to receive data addresses and commands from said host computer and transmit corrected data to said host computer to insure an uninterrupted flow of data from said controller to said host computer.

Lurking in the above claim is the following clause:

> . . . detecting errors in said assembled data **after** correction of said data . . .

MediaTek maintained that its device did not infringe because it performed operations in the opposite sequence — detecting errors *before* correction of the data. Actually, it was a little more complicated than that.

Illustrated in Figure 8–5 (a), the MediaTek device first performed a CRC check (error detection). It then performed the Reed-Solomon algorithm (error correction). However, because the Reed-Solomon algorithm may have made changes to the data, the MediaTek device performed a second operation to update the original CRC value and thereby remove the effect of any error correction. MediaTek took the position that this second operation was simply an extra step, not contemplated by the patent-in-suit. Thus, it argued that its device performed error detection before error correction and not after.

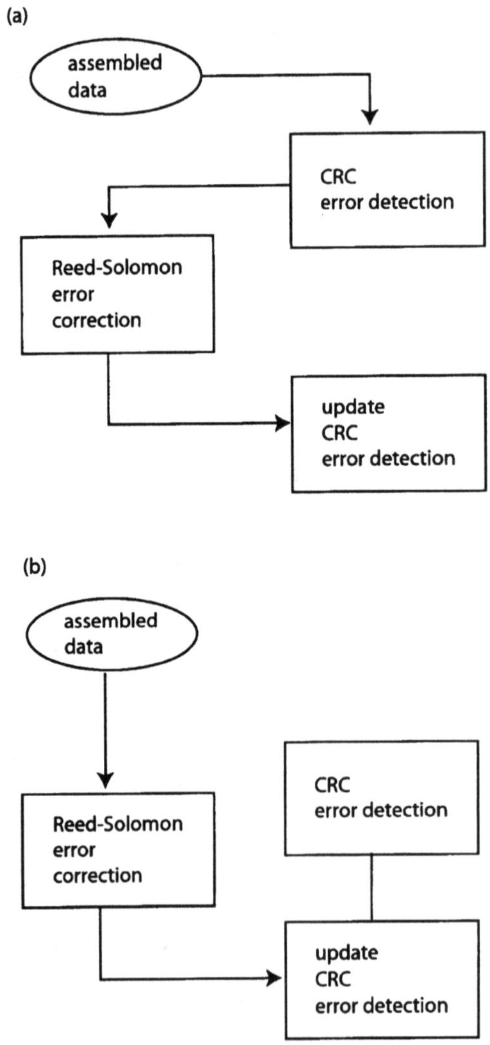

FIGURE 8–5.

Oak Technology viewed MediaTek's analysis as a sham. Because the CRC error detection was not *completed* until after error correction, it argued that MediaTek's device performed error detection correction *after* error correction and was therefore well within the scope of the patent claims. Figure 8–5 (b) illustrates Oak Technology's position.

[3] How the Federal Circuit Construed the "After" Limitation

The court had little difficulty with the term "after." The difficulty, if any, was determining after *what?* Had the MediaTek device performed a full, second CRC operation after Reed-Solomon error correction, then Oak Technology would have had a winning argument. It could then have treated the first CRC operation as superfluous and shown that the accused device met the literal language of the claim: by performing error correction first and then the (second) CRC operation. However, in this case the second CRC operation was merely a touch-up correction of the first CRC results. Thus, the court treated the second operation as superfluous. With that resolved, the court concluded that the accused device did not meet the "check-after-correction" language of the claim.

If you find all of this a bit confusing, consider this easier example. Assume your neighbor's claim says, "cut your lawn; then paint your house after cutting the lawn." To avoid the claim you decide to paint your house first, then cut your lawn. That would seem to be a pretty good strategy for avoiding literal infringement. However, in cutting your lawn you get a few grass clippings on your freshly painted house, requiring you to do a little last-minute scraping and touch-up work on the paint job after the lawn cutting is completed. Your neighbor watches all of this from his dining room window and sues for infringement. Are you guilty of "painting your house" after cutting the lawn? Or, is your touch-up work on the paint job a separate act, distinct from the earlier house painting. That, in essence, is what the court had to decide. In the *Oak Technology* case it decided that house painting and touch-up work are separate acts.

Anyone who has ever painted a house will appreciate that any difference between painting and touch-up is a matter of debate. One man's paint job is another man's touch-up. In the *Oak Technology* case, however, the court found guidance in the patent specification. Unfortunately for Oak Technology, its specification did not disclose the possibility that error detection might begin before error correction was completed. (It did not contemplate that house painting might commence before lawn mowing and finish thereafter.) As the court put it,

> . . . the only embodiment described in the '715 patent always performs error correction before performing CRC error detection. There is no mention in the '715 patent of any embodiments where the sequence of operations is reversed, or where error detection begins before error correction has been completed.[89]

[89] Oak Technology, Inc. v. International Trade Comm'n 248 F.3d 1316, 1328 (Fed. Cir. 2001).

[4] When Claiming Temporal Elements, Draft the Specification for Flexible Interpretation

Temporal terms and sequence-defining terms, such as "before" and "after," wield great power. The wise practitioner uses them with care. Just as we saw with simple conjunctive terms, like "or," these sequence-defining prepositions can create a trap for the unwary. In this case, the trap is using serial or sequential thinking when an equally plausible approach uses parallel or nonsequential thinking. If a preferred embodiment of the invention performs steps (a), (b), and (c) in sequential order, consider alternate embodiments in which the order of these steps is changed, and in which one or more of the steps are performed concurrently (in parallel). If you practice seeing different temporal possibilities you will soon find yourself writing specifications and claims that are more robust and easier for a court to construe in your client's favor.

For an easy way to begin, learn to spot yourself using sequence-implying terms like "before" and "after" in the claims you draft. Ask yourself if you need these terms at all. While the preferred embodiment may operate in a certain temporal sequence, consider other alternatives that may not require adherence to the same sequence. Often a claim can be made more robust by simply leaving out the sequence-implying term.

If you do need to use a sequence-implying term, then you will want to give thought to how you delineate when one step ends and the next step begins. One place to do that is in the patent specification. In the *Oak Technology* case, for example, the patent specification described the Reed-Solomon error correction step as being completed before the CRC error detecting began. Thus, the court construing the limitation (". . . detecting errors in said assembled data after correction of said data . . .") had no choice but to construe these steps as a serialized sequence. If the specification had also taught that the CRC error-detecting step could be initiated before or during the Reed-Solomon step, then Oak Technology's claim interpretation might have carried the day.

[D] Another Temporal Example: "Prior To" What?

In the preceding section, we considered a claim that employed the temporal term "after." In this section we consider another example of a temporal claim. This time, the patent specification helped the patentee's claim construction. The patent involves computer virus protection.

In an IBM research paper presented at the 5th Virus Bulletin International Conference, Boston, September 20-22, 1995, authors Steve R. White, Jeffrey O. Kephart, and David M. Chess report that:

> Over the past decade, computer viruses have gone from an academic curiosity to a persistent, worldwide problem. Viruses can be written for, and spread on, virtually any computing platform. While there have been a few large-scale network-based incidents to date the more significant problem has been on

microcomputers. Viruses are an ongoing, persistent, worldwide problem on every popular microcomputing platform.[90]

Indeed, many microcomputer users learned about viruses firsthand when news spread in March 1992 of a potent computer virus, called "Michaelangelo," that was programmed to attack computers around the globe on March 6, 1992. Six months after the Michaelangelo attack, in September 1992, three inventors from Monroe, Michigan, applied for a patent on their solution to the computer virus problem. Their patent, U.S. patent 5,319,776,[91] was entitled, "In Transit Detection of Computer Virus With Safeguard." The inventors assigned the patent to their company, Hilgrave Corporation, a software company located in Monroe, Michigan.

The Hilgrave patent described a computer virus detection solution. It would scan a digital data file for viruses as the file was transferred to a storage medium. If the software detected a virus prior to storing the file, it automatically blocked storage of the file. The software could be used, for example, to scan a file for viruses as the file was transferred from a floppy disk to a hard disk of a computer system, or as the file was transferred over the Internet from one computer system to a storage medium of another computer system.

Approximately a year after the Hilgrave patent issued, Microsoft released its hugely popular operating system, Windows 95 in August of 1995. By early 1996 a somewhat buggy virus known as "Boza," arrived on the scene to become the first virus to specifically target Windows 95. That same year the "Concept" virus emerged and infected many Microsoft Word documents. Concept was the first virus to exploit the Word macro language. Also that year, another macro virus known as "Laroux" began infecting Excel spreadsheet files. With the onset of these macro viruses, computer users learned to their dismay that their computers could be attacked by simply opening infected Word documents and Excel spreadsheet files sent to them by their friends and relatives. Millions of computer users were beginning to discover that they had to have virus protection software.

In response, two of the largest purveyors of software tools began shipping thousands of copies of virus protection software. The companies were Symantec, maker of Norton Antivirus products, and McAfee, maker of Virus Scan, Dr. Solomon, and Virex products. These products all claimed to eliminate the threat of virus attack by scanning for and cleaning infected files, even those downloaded via the Internet.

In 1997 Hilgrave filed separate suits for patent infringement against Symantec and against McAfee. Hilgrave asserted that these companies' virus protection software infringed the Hilgrave patent. Both suits resulted in district court decisions adverse to Hilgrave, which were reversed on appeal. Of interest here is the appeal in the Symantec suit. In that suit, the Federal Circuit focused on claim language that

---

[90] White, Kephart & Chess, "Computer Viruses: A Global Perspective," "5th Virus Bulletin International Conference, Boston, September 20–22, 1995, Virus Bulletin Ltd., Abingdon, England, <www.research.ibm.com/antivirus/SciPapers/White/VB95/vb95.distrib.html>.

[91] U.S. patent No. 5,319,776 (issued June 7, 1994).

called for receiving and screening the transferred digital data *prior to storage* on the destination storage medium.

[1] Hilgrave's Claim Recites "Prior to Storage"

The Hilgrave patent included several different styles of claims. An exemplary claim is presented below in which emphasis has been added to highlight some of the operative language that was the focus of the court's review.

> 1. In a system for transferring digital data for storage in a computer storage medium, a method of screening the data as it is being transferred and automatically inhibiting the storage of screened data containing at least one predefined sequence, comprising the steps of:
>
> causing a quantity of digital data resident on a source storage medium to be transferred to a computer system having a destination storage medium;
>
> receiving and screening the transferred digital data **prior to storage** on the destination storage medium to determine if at least one of a plurality of predefined sequences are present in the digital data received; and in response to said screening step:
>
> [a] automatically causing the screened digital data to be stored on said destination storage medium if none of the plurality of predefined sequences are present, and
>
> [b] automatically inhibiting the screened digital data from being stored on said destination storage medium if at least one predefined sequence is present.

[2] Symantec Argues It Does Not Infringe

Symantec mounted its defense by focusing on the claim language, highlighted above, reciting the step of "receiving and screening the transferred digital data **prior to storage** on the destination storage medium." Symantec maintained that its system did not meet these terms because, according to its experts, the Symantec products stored first and then screened for viruses.

Symantec's expert described the sequence of steps performed by Symantec's Norton AntiVirus (NAV) product as follows:

> In this sequence, first (step one) a file is transferred for storage onto the destination storage medium. This transfer includes opening a new file on the storage medium and recording incoming data into the new file. Second (step two), the application causing the transfer makes a request to the operating system to close the file containing the transferred data. Third (step three), the operating system closes the file. Fourth (step four), after the file is closed, the Symantec product invokes the NAV Scan Engine to test the file for the presence of a virus.

Symantec's expert alleged that after the third step and before the fourth step, the file is recorded on the storage medium and accessible to the operating system and other programs — and therefore "stored," and that since this occurs before the file is scanned for viruses, Symantec's products do not infringe.

Hilgrave's expert stated that although he agreed with Symantec's "overview" of how the accused products operated, in his opinion there were critical points in the analysis that did not correspond with the behavior of the NAV as it executed. Hilgrave's expert noted that the accused products imposed a barrier in the computer system's file system that prevented all programs and the operating system from accessing the transferred file until after it was processed and screened for viruses. Thus, Hilgrave's expert disputed that the transferred file became accessible to the operating system and other programs between steps three and four.

The positions taken by the respective parties thus raised the question of what the term "storage" in the language "prior to storage" means. Hilgrave took the position that "storage" occurred when the incoming digital data was sufficiently present on the destination storage medium, and accessible by the operating system or other programs, so that any viruses contained in the data could spread and infect the computer system. Symantec took the position that "storage" should be construed to occur when the data became physically present (i.e., magnetically recorded) on the storage medium.

[3] The Court Relies on the Specification in Choosing the Hilgrave Construction

To decide which claim construction was correct, the Federal Circuit Court of Appeals looked to the patent specification. It found:

> The '776 patent distinguishes prior art virus scanning programs because they "do not automatically prevent the virus from being stored on the medium in the first place, hence they cannot totally prevent the virus from attacking or spreading." '776 patent, col. 1, ll. 51-54. Thus, "storage" of the virus is identified with the virus's ability to spread and infect the computer system. A virus may not spread or infect the computer system, however, unless it is accessed by the operating system or other programs. Given this, we agree . . . that "storage" occurs "when the incoming digital data [are] sufficiently present on the destination storage medium and accessible by the operating system or other programs so that any viruses contained in the data can spread and infect the computer system."[92]

With this claim construction, the court concluded that the Symantec products did receive and screen the transferred digital data prior to storage on the destination storage medium.

[4] The Specification Is the Claim Drafter's Friend

Unlike the outcome in *Oak Technology,* discussed in § 8.08 [B]–[B][4] above, the outcome in *Hilgrave* was ultimately favorable to the patentee

[92] Hilgrave Corp. v. Symantec Corp., 265 F.3d 1336, 1342 (Fed. Cir. 2001).

because the patent specification contained support for the patentee's claim interpretation.

Note that the court construed "storage" in light of the problem the invention was designed to address, namely the spread of computer viruses. The court thus tied the term "storage" to the invention's ability to prevent the virus from attacking or spreading. Being "accessible by the operating system" of the computer carried more claim construction weight than merely being "magnetically recorded," because the former definition related to the problem being addressed, whereas the latter definition did not.

Accordingly, one lesson to extract from this case is to keep the purpose and objectives of the invention in mind when selecting claim language and when explaining the invention's configuration and operation in the specification.

Chapter 15

INTEGRATING SOFTWARE PATENTS WITH INDUSTRY STANDARDS

Page 689, Add after end of Chapter 14:

§ 15.01 WHEN SOFTWARE PATENTS AND INDUSTRY STANDARDS COLLIDE

For some, the war against software patents is not over. In 1994, when the first edition of this book was being drafted, much of the software industry believed that software patents were inherently evil. Some still do. Some see software patents as a tar pit, into which even the mightiest software companies will eventually sink into an oily and suffocating demise. So far, that has not happened. On the contrary, mighty software companies — Microsoft, Oracle, Sun, Adobe, IBM, and many others — have prospered in the software patent climate. There is little evidence that these companies are doomed to be discovered, centuries from now, as so many forgotten carcasses — mastodons in the tar pit of the information age.

Still, there are those who believe that the constraints imposed on the software industry by patent law — and indeed by any law — are an affront to the industry's free-spirited character. This view is not wrong either. But that is the nature of evolution. The constraints required by an evolving society will often supplant the freedoms enjoyed by an earlier society. Certainly, the Native American people found themselves trapped in this reality as they watched the free expanse of their North American continent being carved up by the railroads two centuries ago.

Society evolves through unseen forces imposed by the constant pressure of commerce — economist Adam Smith called it the "invisible hand." Software patents are simply tools. It is the press of commerce that causes society to use those tools. Just as the economy seems to grow in largely unpredictable ways, so too does the body of software patents. You can study software patent filing statistics all you want and still be in no position to predict the next "killer application," just as you can study mountains of old Wall Street Journals and still be in no position to predict what stock prices will do tomorrow. In both cases you are more or less destined to simply sit back and watch.

The body of software patents will inevitably grow, as it has already grown, under the constant pressure of commerce that we are powerless to control. Nevertheless, there are those who can see a potential for great good if the course of this growth can be controlled — and a potential for great harm if it cannot. The software industry, like other industries, recognizes that it can benefit by cooperating to develop industry standards. Perhaps there is no better case study to explore industry standards than the Internet. The Internet is unquestionably the most unifying presence in the software industry today. The Internet would not exist today had the software industry been unable to agree to support industry standards, like the TCP/IP protocol by which information is packaged and shipped.

Some see software patents as an inherent threat to the Internet standardization process. The threat is palpable because we have all experienced a get-rich-quick schemer who would lure the world into driving on the right-hand side of the road (or the left-hand side) and then spring forth, patent in hand, claiming to own a monopoly on placing the steering wheel on the left side of the vehicle (or right).

§ 15.02 CASE STUDY: THE WORLD WIDE WEB CONSORTIUM

In October 1994 Tim Berners-Lee founded the World Wide Web Consortium or W3C. Many will recognize Tim Berners-Lee as the inventor of the World Wide Web. Founded to promote interoperability and to foster open discussion, the W3C quickly attracted an impressive membership from all over the world.

Among its long-term goals, the W3C wants to make the Web accessible to all, devoid of cultural, educational, physical, or geographic barriers. It wants to mold the Web into a software environment that will permit each user to make the best use of the resources available, while giving careful consideration to the social issues raised by this technology. To achieve these goals, the W3C is organized primarily to (a) identify technical requirements that must be satisfied, (b) design Web technologies to address these requirements, and (c) promote standardization. It is this last role that has put the W3C in the software patent limelight. To promote technological standardization, the W3C has recognized that there may be a need to control software patents through self-regulation and licensing.

The W3C has quite a challenge ahead of it. Its membership is diverse (see subsection 15.02 [A] below). Some of its members are extremely powerful and are often observed at opposite ends of the tug-of-war rope: take Microsoft and Sun Microsytems, for instance. Other W3C members, while perhaps less active in pulling on the rope, are inevitably caught up in the struggle between industry standards and proprietary rights. It is a game of three-dimensional chess. It is quite possible that some companies have joined the W3C just to promote a standard that everyone should drive, on the right-hand side, down a road that just happens to pass under a toll gate operated by their patent trial counsel.

[A] W3C Members

The World Wide Web Consortium (W3C) has over five hundred members. The list is impressive. It contains members in diverse fields ranging from computer hardware and software companies, to financial institutions, telecommunications companies, research foundations, dot-com e-businesses, universities, consumer products companies, book publishers, writers, and even government agencies. The complete list may be found on the W3C Web site at <www.w3.org/Consortium/Member/List>. The following pages present an abridged list that will give the flavor of the influence this consortium enjoys. See if your company or client is on the list. If not, check the W3C Web site.

[1] Partial List of W3C Members

Adobe Systems Inc.
Agfa-Gevaert N. V.
Alcatel
America Online, Inc.
American Express
Apple Computer, Inc.
Ask Jeeves, Inc.
AT&T
Autodesk, Inc.
The Boeing Company
University of Bologna
University of Bristol
British Broadcasting Corporation
Canon, Inc.
Cerisent Corporation
CERN
ChevronTexaco
Chinese University of Hong Kong
Cisco Systems
CITIBANK, N.A.
Citrix Systems (Cambridge) Ltd.
Commerce One
CommerceNet
Compaq Computer Corporation
Computer Associates
Corel Corporation
DaimlerChrysler Research and Technology
Defense Information Systems Agency (DISA)
DoubleClick
Eastman Kodak Company
Ecole Mohammadia d'Ingenieurs Rabat (EMI)
École Nationale Supérieure d'Informatique et de Mathématiques Appliquées (ENSIMAG)
University of Edinburgh (HCRC Language Technology Group)
Electricité de France
Electronic Data System (EDS)
ERICSSON
Fermi National Accelerator Laboratory
Fidelity Investments
Fondazione Ugo Bordoni
Forschungszentrum Informatik (FZI)
Foundation for Research and Technology–Hellas (FORTH)
France Telecom
Fraunhofer Gesellschaft
Fujitsu Limited
General Magic, Inc.
German Research Center for Artificial Intelligence (DFKI) Gmbh
University of Hawaii
The Hebrew University of Jerusalem
Hewlett Packard Company
Hitachi, Ltd.
Honda Motor Co., Ltd
Hong Kong Jockey Club
Hong Kong Productivity Council
Hong Kong University of Science & Technology
HTML Writers Guild, Inc.
IBM Corporation
IEEE Computer Society
Information Broadcasting Laboratories, Inc. (IB Labs)
Institut Für Halbleiterphysik
Institut National de Recherche en Informatique et en Automatique (INRIA)
Internet Academy, Inc.
Internet Association Japan (IA Japan)
Internet Business Japan, Inc.
Internet Technology Research Committee (ITRC)
Interoperability Technology Association for Information Processing, Japan
J-Phone Tokyo Co., Ltd.
Japan Broadcasting Corporation (NHK)
Keio University

University of Kent at Canterbury
Lawrence Berkeley National Laboratory
Lernout & Hauspie
Library of Congress
Los Alamos National Laboratory
Lucent Technologies
Macromedia
Maryland Information and Network Dynamics Lab at the University of Maryland
Massachusetts Institute of Technology (MIT)
Massachusetts Medical Society
Matsushita Electric Industrial Co., Ltd. (MEI)
Merrill Lynch
Metropolitan Police Service
Microsoft Corporation
Millennium Pharmaceuticals
MITRE Corporation
Mitsubishi Electric Corporation
Motorola
NASA Ames Research Center
National Computerization Agency
National Institute of Standards and Technology (NIST)
National Library of Australia
National Office for the Information Economy
National Research Council Canada
National Security Agency (NSA)
NATO Consultation, Command and Control Agency
NEC Corporation
NHS (National Health Service, UK)
Nippon Telegraph & Telephone Corp (NTT)
Nisus, Inc.
Nokia
Nortel Networks
Norwegian Broadcasting Corporation (NRK)
Novell, Inc.
NTT DoCoMo
Nuance Communications
O'Reilly & Associates, Inc.
Organization for the Advancement of Structured Information Standards (OASIS)
Object Management Group, Inc. (OMG)
OCLC (Online Computer Library Center, Inc.)
Omnitel-Vodafone
Oracle Corporation
Oxford Brookes University
Philips Electronic N.V.
PureEdge Solutions
Qualcomm Inc.
Rational Software Corporation
RealNetworks
Recording for the Blind & Dyslexic
Reed Elsevier
Rogue Wave Software
Royal KPN NV
Royal Melbourne Institute of Technology
Royal National Institute for the Blind (RNIB)
Sanyo Electric Company Ltd.
SAP AG
Charles Schwab & Co., Inc.
SHARE, Inc.
Sharp Corporation
Siemens AG
Software & Information Industry Association (SIIA)
Software AG
Sony Corporation
University of Southampton
Speech Works International, Inc.
Spyglass, Inc.
Stanford University
Sun Microsystems, Inc.
Sybase, Inc.
Toshiba Corporation
U.S. National Library of Medicine

Uniform Code Council, Inc.
Unisys Corporation
United States Environmental Protection Agency (EPA)
Università Commerciale "Luigi Bocconi"
University of Helsinki
VeriSign, Inc.
Western Australian Department of Commerce and Trade/Office of Information and Communications
WinWriters
Wolfram Research, Inc.
Xerox Corporation

[B] The Patent Policy Project

For some time, a W3C working group known as the Patent Policy working group has been working on a standardization project that is fundamentally different from most technological standard-defining projects. This group is trying to draft policies by which W3C members can cooperate to share software patent rights, if that would help promote other technological standards. Periodically, the group publishes its efforts in the form of a Patent Policy document. Like other standard-defining groups, these published documents are intended to serve as a vehicle for discussion and ultimately for W3C member acceptance.

On February 26, 2002, the Patent Policy working group published its Royalty-Free Patent Policy, the most recent draft as of this writing. Although this draft is still a work in progress, the notes accompanying the February 26 draft suggest that the next draft will probably be the final one. After that the document is expected to mature into a Proposed Recommendation. In the W3C standards creation process, "working notes" mature into "proposed recommendations," which mature into official "recommendations." For a better understanding of the entire standards-creation process, see § 15.04[A]. While the Royalty-Free Patent Policy currently contemplates a royalty-free relationship among the W3C members, a number of members in the past believed (and may still believe) that a royalty-bearing license option should be included in the policy. Such a royalty-bearing provision was included in prior versions of the working document, but those provisions were dropped in the February 26 draft.

In addition to licensing provisions, the draft also prescribes an assortment of rules requiring working group members to notify each other if they are planning to claim a proprietary patent position that would block a W3C recommendation from being implemented.

[1] Royalty-Free License

The basic terms of the royalty-free license are as follows:

> A Royalty-Free license shall mean a non-assignable, non-sublicensable license to make, have made, use, have used, sell, have sold, offer to sell,

> import, and distribute and dispose of implementations of the Recommendation that:
>
> 1. shall be available to all implementers of the specification worldwide, whether or not they are W3C Members;
>
> 2. shall extend to all Essential Claims owned or controlled by the licensor and its Affiliates;
>
> 3. may be limited to implementations of the Recommendation, and to what is required by the Recommendation;
>
> 4. may be conditioned on a grant of a reciprocal RF license (as defined in this policy) to all Essential Claims owned or controlled by the licensee. A reciprocal license may be required to be available to all, and a reciprocal license may itself be conditioned on a further reciprocal license from all.
>
> 5. may not be conditioned on payment of royalties, fees or other consideration;
>
> 6. may be suspended with respect to any licensee when licensor is sued by licensee for infringement of patents used to implement any W3C Recommendation;
>
> 7. may not impose any further conditions or restrictions on the use of any technology, intellectual property rights, or other restrictions on behavior of the licensee, but may include reasonable, customary terms relating to operation or maintenance of the license relationship such as the following: choice of law and dispute resolution;
>
> 8. shall not be considered accepted by an implementer who manifests an intent not to accept the terms of the Royalty-Free license as offered by the licensor.[1]

The trigger for this royalty-free license is something called an "essential claim." The draft defines an essential claim as one that would "necessarily be infringed" by an implementation of a recommendation. Under the royalty-free provisions, members are to receive a royalty-free license under such essential claims. That would seem to cover quite a lot. There are time limits, however, governing what claims will get corralled as essential claims. A claim is not branded an "essential claim" unless it appears in a patent or patent application that has an effective filing date within one year and one day after the first public working draft was published. The following excerpt shows the scope of the "essential claim" concept:

> "Essential Claims" shall mean all claims in any patent or patent application with an effective filing date within one year and one day after the publication of the first public Working Draft, in any jurisdiction in the world, that a Member (or a licensor or licensee, with reference to entities other than

---

[1] Royalty-Free Patent Policy, Patent Policy Working Group, World Wide Web Consortium, W3C Working Draft, February 26, 2002, <www.w3.org/TR/2002/WD-patent-policy-20020226>.

> Members) owns, or under which a Member (or a licensor or licensee) has the right to grant licenses without obligation of payment or other consideration to an unrelated third party, that would necessarily be infringed by implementation of the Recommendation. A claim is necessarily infringed hereunder only when it is not possible to avoid infringing it because there is no non-infringing alternative for implementing the required portions of the Recommendation. Existence of a non-infringing alternative shall be judged based on the state-of-the-art at the time the specification becomes a Recommendation.[2]

You might be wondering, what about enabling technologies that are necessary to make or use a product that conforms to the recommendation, but that are not expressly set forth in the recommendation. Would claims to such enabling technologies be considered "essential claims"? For example, what if your client makes an operating system or a compiler that is used to make a product that conforms to a W3C Recommendation, and someone has a patent covering that operating system or compiler? Don't count on getting a royalty-free license. The Royalty-Free Patent Policy expressly excludes claims to such enabling technologies from the "essential claims" definition.

There are other exceptions to the "essential claims" definition as well. If your client is a member of the W3C, you should check the W3C Web site for the latest, full definition of "essential claims" and the claims excluded from that definition.

[2] Disclosure Requirements of the W3C Patent Policy

Patent applications begin their life in a veil of secrecy. In the United States, patent applications are maintained by the Patent Office in strictest secrecy until 18 months after filing. An applicant who is willing to forego using that U.S. application as a basis for international filing can voluntarily elect to have his or her application remain secret during the entire time the application is pending. The rules governing secrecy, which have grown rather complicated of late, are set forth in the next section.

Although in most cases patent application secrecy is short lived (18 months), that secrecy could nevertheless present problems should an unwitting working group agree to adopt standards that were actually covered by a nondisclosed pending patent application, or even covered by an undiscovered issued patent that is buried in a member's patent portfolio. The Patent Policy working group addressed this issue by including a set of disclosure requirements that the W3C members must adhere to. Before getting into those requirements, it may be helpful to review exactly how the veil of secrecy actually works under U.S. patent law.

---

[2] Royalty-Free Patent Policy, Patent Policy Working Group, World Wide Web Consortium, W3C Working Draft, February 26, 2002, <www.w3.org/TR/2002/WD-patent-policy-20020226>.

[a] Confidential Status of Applications; Publication of Patent Applications — 35 U.S.C. § 122

The U.S. patent laws set forth a somewhat complicated roadmap that directs how secrecy of pending patent applications may be maintained. The following became law as a result of the American Inventors Protection Act of 1999:[3]

(a) Confidentiality —

Except as provided in subsection (b), applications for patents shall be kept in confidence by the Patent and Trademark Office and no information concerning the same given without authority of the applicant or owner unless necessary to carry out the provisions of an Act of Congress or in such special circumstances as may be determined by the Director.

(b) Publication —

(1) In general —

(A)

Subject to paragraph (2), each application for a patent shall be published, in accordance with procedures determined by the Director, promptly after the expiration of a period of 18 months from the earliest filing date for which a benefit is sought under this title. At the request of the applicant, an application may be published earlier than the end of such 18-month period.

(B)

No information concerning published patent applications shall be made available to the public except as the Director determines.

(C)

Notwithstanding any other provision of law, a determination by the Director to release or not to release information concerning a published patent application shall be final and nonreviewable.

(2) Exceptions —

(A)

An application shall not be published if that application is —

(i)
no longer pending;
(ii)
subject to a secrecy order under section 181 of this title;
(iii)
a provisional application filed under section 111(b) of this title; or
(iv)
an application for a design patent filed under chapter 16 of this title.

---

[3] Pub. L. No. 106-113, § 4001, (November 29, 1999).

(B)

(i)

If an applicant makes a request upon filing, certifying that the invention disclosed in the application has not and will not be the subject of an application filed in another country, or under a multilateral international agreement, that requires publication of applications 18 months after filing, the application shall not be published as provided in paragraph (1).

(ii)

An applicant may rescind a request made under clause (i) at any time.

(iii)

An applicant who has made a request under clause (i) but who subsequently files, in a foreign country or under a multilateral international agreement specified in clause (i), an application directed to the invention disclosed in the application filed in the Patent and Trademark Office, shall notify the Director of such filing not later than 45 days after the date of the filing of such foreign or international application. A failure of the applicant to provide such notice within the prescribed period shall result in the application being regarded as abandoned, unless it is shown to the satisfaction of the Director that the delay in submitting the notice was unintentional.

(iv)

If an applicant rescinds a request made under clause (i) or notifies the Director that an application was filed in a foreign country or under a multilateral international agreement specified in clause (i), the application shall be published in accordance with the provisions of paragraph (1) on or as soon as is practical after the date that is specified in clause (i).

(v)

If an applicant has filed applications in one or more foreign countries, directly or through a multilateral international agreement, and such foreign filed applications corresponding to an application filed in the Patent and Trademark Office or the description of the invention in such foreign filed applications is less extensive than the application or description of the invention in the application filed in the Patent and Trademark Office, the applicant may submit a redacted copy of the application filed in the Patent and Trademark Office eliminating any part or description of the invention in such application that is not also contained in any of the corresponding applications filed in a foreign country. The Director may only publish the redacted copy of the application unless the redacted copy of the application is not received

> within 16 months after the earliest effective filing date for which a benefit is sought under this title. The provisions of section 154(d) shall not apply to a claim if the description of the invention published in the redacted application filed under this clause with respect to the claim does not enable a person skilled in the art to make and use the subject matter of the claim.[4]

[b] Dealing With Secrecy in an Open Standards World

To guard working group members from being unwittingly duped into developing and adopting a recommendation that would embroil them in patent infringement litigation, the Patent Policy working group has proposed a disclosure obligation. The disclosure obligation is ongoing, beginning when a standard-forming working group makes a call for participation. As a working document proceeds through its various stages of scrutiny and approval (see § 15.04[A] for a description of these stages), the document will include a call for disclosure of any patents or patent applications that a working group member is aware of that may contain "essential claims," as that term is defined by the Patent Policy (see § 15.02 [B][1] for definition).

Because complete disclosure may not be possible until later in the process, when the design is more complete, the Patent Policy contemplates disclosure at each milestone of the standards-creation process. The disclosure obligation terminates once a formal recommendation is published or when the working group terminates. The Patent Policy requires reasonable disclosure compliance. Members are not required to conduct patent searches, but members are required to disclose when they have actual knowledge of likely essential claims with respect to a specification.

[3] Excluding Key Patents From Royalty-Free License

Membership in the W3C working group is voluntary. While a working group member is strongly encouraged to comply with the royalty-free licensing and disclosure obligations, the Patent Policy is realistic. Some working group members may have business reasons for either resigning from the working group, or continuing to participate but withdrawing specific patents from the royalty-free licensing commitment. Therefore, under the Patent Policy, a working group member may resign from the working group within 60 days after publication of a requirements document and have no further obligation under the licensing commitments. If that member wishes to resign after the 60-day time interval, that member is considered bound only to license claims that are considered essential — as of the state of the latest working document.

A working group member who wishes to remain in the group may also have certain patents excluded from the royalty-free licensing commitment by giving

---

[4] 35 U.S.C. § 122.

notice. To do this the member must give notice within 60 days after the working group publishes its requirements document. A working group member can even exclude "essential claims" from the royalty-free licensing obligation by giving notice within 60 days after the "last call" working draft is published.

Being able to exclude "essential claims" that are "necessarily infringed" by implementation of the recommendation, seems to open a loophole that could unravel the entire open-standards effort. Whether that will happen in practice remains to be seen. An earlier draft of the Patent Policy contained a licensing provision that many considered to be far more damaging to the open-standards movement. It was called the RAND provision.

§ 15.03 THE RAND PROVISIONS — WITHDRAWN FROM THE PATENT POLICY

In the working drafts of the Patent Policy prior to the February 26, 2002 draft, patent holders had the option to offer either a royalty-free license or a royalty-bearing license. The royalty-bearing license required the licensing terms to be "reasonable and non-discriminatory," hence earning the acronym "RAND." The RAND provisions lit a conflagration of complaints among open-standard supporters and journalists who cover Internet topics. A cogent argument was made that the W3C should not give patent holders the opportunity to choose a royalty-bearing license by default:

> The W3C has recognised the pressures from (some of) its members to be able to exploit the potentially lucrative Internet-related patents they have been accumulating. There appears to be a resignation that it may be better for the W3C to promote standards that have non-free conditions attached rather than to receive no consensus on potential recommendations.
>
> However by doing this the W3C is diminishing the significant tool they have to encourage royalty-free licensing: their official stamp of approval on Internet technologies and credit to the companies that provide those technologies. The support of the W3C is an important factor for a web-based standard to achieve dominance. A company might be willing to provide their intellectual property on royalty-free terms to receive W3C approval and thus an increasing chance for their sponsored standard to become widely adopted. Now those same companies may think they can get the best of both worlds: A W3C recommendation and the reserved right to charge licensing fees in the future.[5]

In response to such arguments, the Patent Policy drafting committee dropped the RAND provisions from the February 26, 2002 Patent Policy draft.

[5] Warner, A., "W3C and the Promotion of Fee-based Standards for the Web," Archive of the Original 28 September Document that Sparked the W3C Patent Policy Debate, <www.openphd.net/W3C_Patent_Policy/28_Sept_Document/>.

§ 15.04 CREATING INDUSTRY STANDARDS IN AN INDUSTRY THAT ENDORSES PATENTS

The World Wide Web Consortium members have expended considerable effort promulgating industry-wide software patent licensing standards. Their efforts are important here for two reasons. First, the W3C Patent Policy may impose duties upon its members who own software patents. Second, the W3C Patent Policy gives us a framework for developing and promoting industry-wide standards in fields outside the World Wide Web. An industry wishing to promote industry standards in home automation, for example, might use the W3C Patent Policy as a framework for developing their own patent policy.

The W3C Web site is extensive, which should come as no surprise, given its founder and director is none other than Tim Berners-Lee, inventor of the World Wide Web. As an entry point to learning about the W3C, you might begin at <www.w3.org/Consortium/#w3c-process>, a Web page that gives a good overview of the organization with many hyperlinks leading you to many details. For a thumbnail sketch of the W3C approach to developing standards, the organization's multi-level technical report structure is a good place to begin.

[A] W3C Technical Reports

The W3C defines several different levels of technical reports that basically track the process by which a submitted idea matures into a recommendation for widespread adoption. This very procedure is also being followed by the Patent Policy working group. Figure 15–1 illustrates this process and the technical reports promulgated at each stage. You will need a basic understanding of this process to interpret your client's disclosure and licensing obligations as a W3C member.

Any W3C member can submit an idea for consideration as a recommended standard. The W3C calls such submissions "Notes." A Note is simply a dated, public record of an idea. The W3C makes no commitment that the idea will be pursued. If the W3C does decide to pursue the idea, a "Working Draft" document is prepared. The Working Draft reveals a work in process of a working group that has undertaken to develop the idea. Members of the working group use the Working Document to preserve their thoughts and as a vehicle for further discussion. In fact, the W3C Patent Policy that gave rise to the disclosure and licensing obligations of W3C members began as a Working Draft of the Patent Policy working group. Because the Working Draft is a work in process, it does not necessarily reflect consensus among members of the working group.

Once the working group is satisfied that the Working Document is ready for public consumption, the Working Document is transformed into a "Candidate Recommendation." The Candidate Recommendation represents the stage at which members outside the working group are invited to provide technical comments on how the recommendation should be implemented. After sufficient opportunity to receive and digest these technical comments, the Candidate Recommendation re-

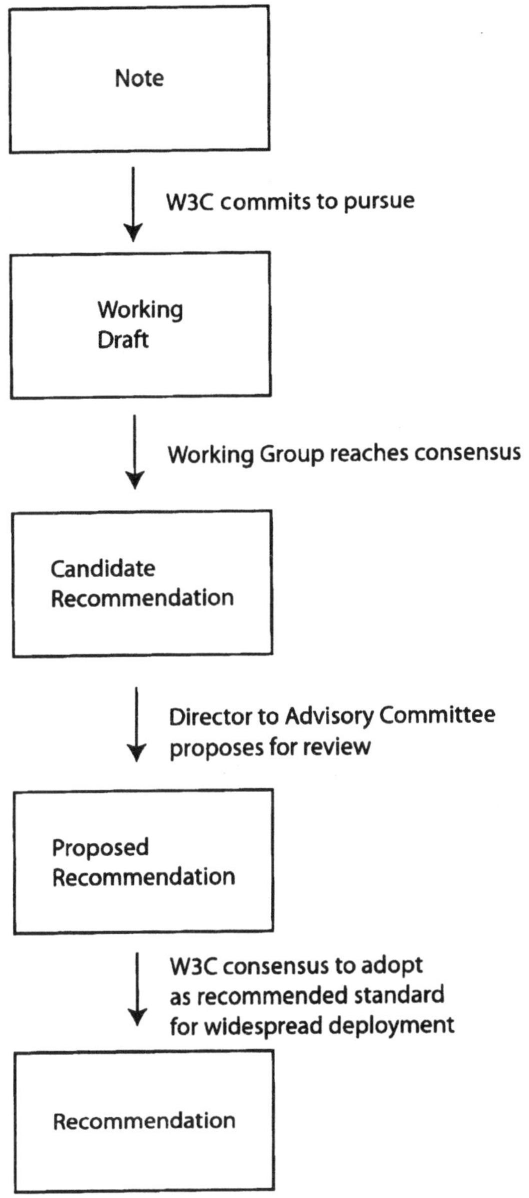

FIGURE 15–1.

ceives scrutiny of the Director to the Advisory Committee. If the Director approves, the Candidate Recommendation matures into a "Proposed Recommendation," the final stage prior to official adoption.

For a Proposed Recommendation each member of the Advisory Committee is given at least four weeks to review the recommendation and vote on it, with comment. Based on the vote, the Proposed Recommendation may be approved (possibly with minor changes), returned to the working group for further development, or rejected. Each member of the W3C is entitled to one seat on the Advisory Committee; thus, this vote represents the consensus within the W3C. Upon adoption, the W3C promulgates the final document as a "Recommendation" that it considers suitable for widespread adoption.

§ 15.05 REPRESENTING A CLIENT WHO IS A MEMBER OF AN INDUSTRY STANDARDS CONSORTIUM

As a member of W3C, your client has certain obligations that may have an impact on its patent strategy. Specifically, it may have a duty to disclose certain information concerning invention disclosures, patent applications, and issued patents the company may own or have knowledge of. If it is represented on a working group it will also need to monitor the proposed standards promulgated by that group very closely, so that it can exclude strategic patents that it does not want to be subject to the royalty-free license.

[A] Meeting the Disclosure Obligations

Disclosure obligations under the W3C Patent Policy arise when "disclosure requests" are promulgated. Disclosure requests may be made by embedding them within a "status" portion of a working document:

> Disclosure requests, seeking information described in 4.0, will be included in the "Status of This Document" section of each technical report as it reaches each new maturity level (requirements document, Working Draft, Last Call Working Draft, Candidate Recommendation, Proposed Recommendation, Recommendation).[6]

In response to such a request, your client may have an obligation to identify patents and patent applications that contain "essential claims" that would necessarily be infringed, if the recommendation of the working group is put into practice. Even patents owned by third parties may need to be disclosed, if the third party has made your client aware that it believes the patent contains essential claims, and provided your client is not under confidentiality restrictions that prohibit such disclosure.

Fortunately, your client has no affirmative duty to conduct searches of its patent portfolio to look for patents and applications that might contain essential claims. Nor does the Patent Policy require your client to engage in any analysis of the relationship between the patents and the proposed working group recommendation. The Patent Policy only requires a good faith effort to disclose that which your client has actual knowledge of. Refer to § 15.02[A][2] and to the W3C Web site for further information about the disclosure obligations under the W3C Patent Policy.

---

[6] Royalty-Free Patent Policy, Patent Policy Working Group, World Wide Web Consortium, W3C Working Draft, February 26, 2002, <www.w3.org/TR/2002/WD-patent-policy-20020226/>.

What does your client need to do to meet its disclosure obligations? From a proactive standpoint, there is probably very little your client must do. The Patent Policy bases the disclosure obligation upon good faith disclosure, whether your client has actual knowledge. Your client is not required to conduct patent searches, nor is it required to perform claim analysis of its patents vis-à-vis the working group's proposed recommendation. In most cases the "good faith" compliance is likely to come down to the good faith behavior of a few individuals. It is possible to envision a scenario, however, where a member company might be accused of not disclosing in good faith because the company's working group representative (who would normally receive the disclosure request) has been purposefully sequestered from meaningful access to the company's patent portfolio.

To guard against being accused under this scenario, corporate patent counsel may want to conduct periodic meetings with the company's working group delegate. Because some of the exclusionary rules, discussed in § 15.05[B] have a 60-day time period for response, such meetings between group delegate and patent counsel might be initiated in response to publication by the W3C of a new working draft. Corporate patent counsel may therefore ask to be placed on the routing list of all new working drafts, to give counsel notice that a meeting should be scheduled.

An alternate approach would be to invite the company's working group delegate to periodic patent disclosure review meetings. Many corporations periodically schedule such meetings to evaluate newly submitted invention disclosures for possible patent protection. Having the working group delegate at such meetings would make the patent filing decision makers more aware of activity within the W3C working group. In addition to helping meet the W3C disclosure requirements, such awareness of W3C working group activity could be quite valuable in molding the company's patent portfolio.

[B] Excluding Key Patents From the Royalty-Free License

The W3C Royalty-Free Patent Policy contains a giant loophole that permits a member to electively exclude any of its patents from the royalty-free license constraint. By acting within 60 days of the Working Group's requirements document publication, a member can have key patents excluded from the royalty-free provisions:

> Specific patents may be excluded from the RF licensing commitment by a participant who seeks to remain in the Working Group only if that participant discloses specific patents that will not be licensed on RF terms within 60 days after the publication of the Working Group's requirements document. A participant who excludes patents may continue to participate in the Working Group.[7]

[7] Royalty-Free Patent Policy, Patent Policy Working Group, World Wide Web Consortium, W3C Working Draft, February 26, 2002, <www.w3.org/TR/2002/WD-patent-policy-20020226/>.

The exclusionary option may also be invoked if a member discovers within 60 days of a final Recommendation that claims of its patent have become "essential claims" as a result of subject matter that was not present or apparent in the earlier draft requirements documents. If a party newly joins a working group more than 60 days after a requirements document is published, the new member must invoke the exclusion option, if at all, immediately upon joining the working group.

Open architecture supporters undoubtedly chafe at these exclusionary provisions, as they place the software patent rights of an individual person or company above the interests of the community at large. This is not shortsightedness on the part of the committee that developed the Patent Policy, but rather recognition that membership in the W3C is voluntary and vast. Whereas it might be possible for one or two parties to agree on a royalty-free cross license between them, it becomes geometrically more difficult as the number of parties increases. The W3C currently has over five hundred members. It is unlikely that all can, or should, be expected to agree to grant royalty-free licenses to each other for the sake of the common good.

More important, however, the exclusionary option of the Patent Policy serves a powerful notice function. To have its key patents excluded from the royalty-free license, the owner must identify the patent within 60 days after publication of any working draft or proposed recommendation. Doing so gives the working group the opportunity to restructure its proposed recommended standard to avoid infringing the claims of that patent. While avoiding the claims may not always be possible, the exclusionary option does allow the members of the working group, and the W3C members at large, to proceed with eyes open.

For corporate patent counsel, the exclusionary option under the W3C Patent Policy may require more care and attention than the disclosure obligations discussed in § 15.05[A]. Whereas the disclosure obligations impose no duty to conduct patent searches, the exclusionary option would seem to impose a heavier burden. If key patents are to be excluded from the royalty-free license, then counsel must identify those patents, and utilize the exclusionary option, within 60 days after publication of a requirements document. In effect this requires patent counsel to carefully monitor the published requirements documents to determine if any claims of its client's patents and pending applications would necessarily be infringed by the industry, if the requirements document is adopted as an industry standard.

Doing this can be a tall order, particularly with large corporate clients that have large and diverse patent portfolios. Many corporations maintain database records listing each patent and each pending application in the corporate portfolio. This is certainly good practice. Often corporate patent counsel will include in such database records that identify the company division or product line to which each patent corresponds. Now, to be prepared to invoke the exclusionary option under the W3C Patent Policy, counsel may also wish to include a field in patent database records that identifies any related W3C working group or requirements documents. The royalty-free license provisions of the W3C Patent Policy apply only to those patents having "essential claims" that would necessarily be infringed, if the requirements document is implemented. However, to be on the safe side, it is a good idea to populate your W3C database field where the patent may be potentially relevant—not just where it contains "essential claims."

After constructing the patent database and including any known or suspected W3C relationships, a bit of further data mining may be in order. If one patent in the patent database pertains to the efforts of a W3C working group, there are likely to be others. Thus, counsel may wish to identify all patents that have a potential W3C working group relevance and then construct further database queries that identify other patents that:

- originate from the same division as each relevant W3C patent, or
- pertain to the same product line as each relevant W3C patent, or
- were invented by the same person(s) as each relevant W3C patent.

Upon, identifying patents or applications that may potentially be relevant to a working group document, you will next want to carefully consider whether the patent or application contains claims that are "essential" to implementing the proposed or recommended standard. Do not overlook the possibility that "essential claims" may be drafted at this stage, if the technical disclosure and procedural posture of the patent or application will support additional claims. For example, while the application is still pending, you may have opportunities to amend the claims or to add new claims that would constitute "essential claims," provided the patent specification will support them. If the patent is issued, there may be pending related applications, such as continuation, continuation-in-part, or divisional applications, that can support additional "essential claims." In addition, if the patent has been issued for less than two years, it may be possible to secure "essential claims" through the reissue process.

Ultimately, the decision whether to exclude patents with "essential claims" from the W3C royalty-free license is a business decision that will need to be made at the highest level possible. Failure to timely invoke the exclusionary option could damage valuable patent rights by placing the "essential claims" under royalty-free license restrictions. On the other hand, invoking the exclusionary option will undoubtedly subject your client, and its proprietary patent position, to high levels of industry-wide scrutiny.

What happens if your client invokes the exclusionary option with respect to a patent or application? Other than moral suasion and exposing your client to public scrutiny, there is little the W3C can do. When an "essential claim" is excluded from the royalty-free license, the W3C will convene an ad hoc Patent Advisory Group that will attempt to resolve the impasse. Among the options available to the Patent Advisory Group are:

1. Meet with the patent holder in an effort to persuade the holder to grant a royalty-free license.

2. Instruct the working group to consider designing around the patent.
3. Meet with the patent holder and with working group members to explore whether a reasonable and nondiscriminatory, royalty-bearing license may be worked out.
4. Instruct the working group that it should rescind the recommendation.
5. Terminate the working group.

As options 4 and 5 show, the patent holder holds a trump card in its negotiation with the Patent Advisory Group. Unless a "design around" (option 2) is possible, or unless effective public pressure can be brought to bear, the holder of a key patent can prevent a recommendation from being adopted as an industry standard, and can even cause the working group to be disbanded. Does this therefore mean that the mission of the Royalty-Free Patent Policy is futile? Not necessarily. It is quite possible that the holder of a key patent will benefit greatly by adoption of an industry standard. Thwarting the standards effort might simply cause the industry to take another course that would not benefit the key patent holder as much.

For example, Microsoft has invested considerable effort in promoting its .NET platform for building large, integrated systems. Sun Microsystems has invested equal effort in promoting its Java 2 Enterprise Edition (J2EE) platform for doing the same thing. Given the potential of this enormous market, it is doubtful that Microsoft would invoke the exclusionary provision with respect to a key .NET patent, if that would force the industry to adopt Sun Microsystem's J2EE platform instead. More likely, Microsoft would agree to grant a royalty-free license on that one patent to gain the greater commercial advantage of having its .NET platform adopted as the industry standard.

§ 15.06 FINDING THE INTERSTITIAL PATENT SPACE WITHIN AN INDUSTRY DOMINATED BY STANDARDS

Software patents, like all other patents, have a limited, twenty-year lifespan. Sometimes, the innovations represented by those patents can have an even shorter lifespan—new innovations make old ones obsolete, even before the patents expire. Thus, while industry standards can last forever, those standards will inevitably wax and wane in importance, as markets and lifestyles change. To illustrate, no doubt each of the following recording technologies is the subject of numerous standards. Which of those standards are still important today?

- 78 rpm records
- 45 rpm records
- 33⅓ LP records
- reel-to-reel tape

- 8-track cartridge tape
- cassette tape
- BETA video tape
- VHS video tape
- compact disc (CD)
- compact disc-recordable (CD-R)
- digital audio tape (DAT)
- digital versatile disk (also digital video disk) (DVD)
- digital video disk-recordable (DVD-R)
- digital video disk-read only memory (DVD-RAM)

While some of these technologies, and their respective standards, have (to date) survived the test of time, others are already under museum glass, next to Thomas Edison's recorded wax cylinder of "Mary Had a Little Lamb." Thus, regardless of how important or fundamental a technology may seem, the commercial landscape will always change. Such change inevitably opens up new interstitial space where an innovator can stake a proprietary patent claim within an industry dominated by standards.

To illustrate, you can model the patent landscape as a two-dimensional graph where the technological space covered by a patent portfolio is represented along the horizontal axis and the significance of the portfolio is represented along the vertical axis. See Figure 15–2.

In Figure 15–2, the tall, narrow rectangle represents a single dominant patent that is restricted to a relatively narrow field. The broad rectangle to its right represents a portfolio of patents of more modest coverage (narrower claims) that is spread across a wider technological field. These two rectangles lie side-by-side because they are technologically related.

The field of technology represented by these two rectangles may remain stagnate. In such case there will be little movement in this region of the graph. However, if the field is commercially active, innovators will discover ways of improving the existing technology. That will have the effect of creating new space between the two rectangles, as if the horizontal axis were a rubber sheet that becomes stretched in the local (interstitial) region between the two rectangles.

The effect of an industry-wide royalty-free patent licensing program is to suppress the single dominant patent. Suppressing the dominant patent allows the interstitial space next to it to stretch more freely, because innovators will be more likely to devote resources knowing they are not going to be sued. Thus, while an industry-wide, royalty-free licensing program may be seen by some as anti-patent, quite the opposite is true.

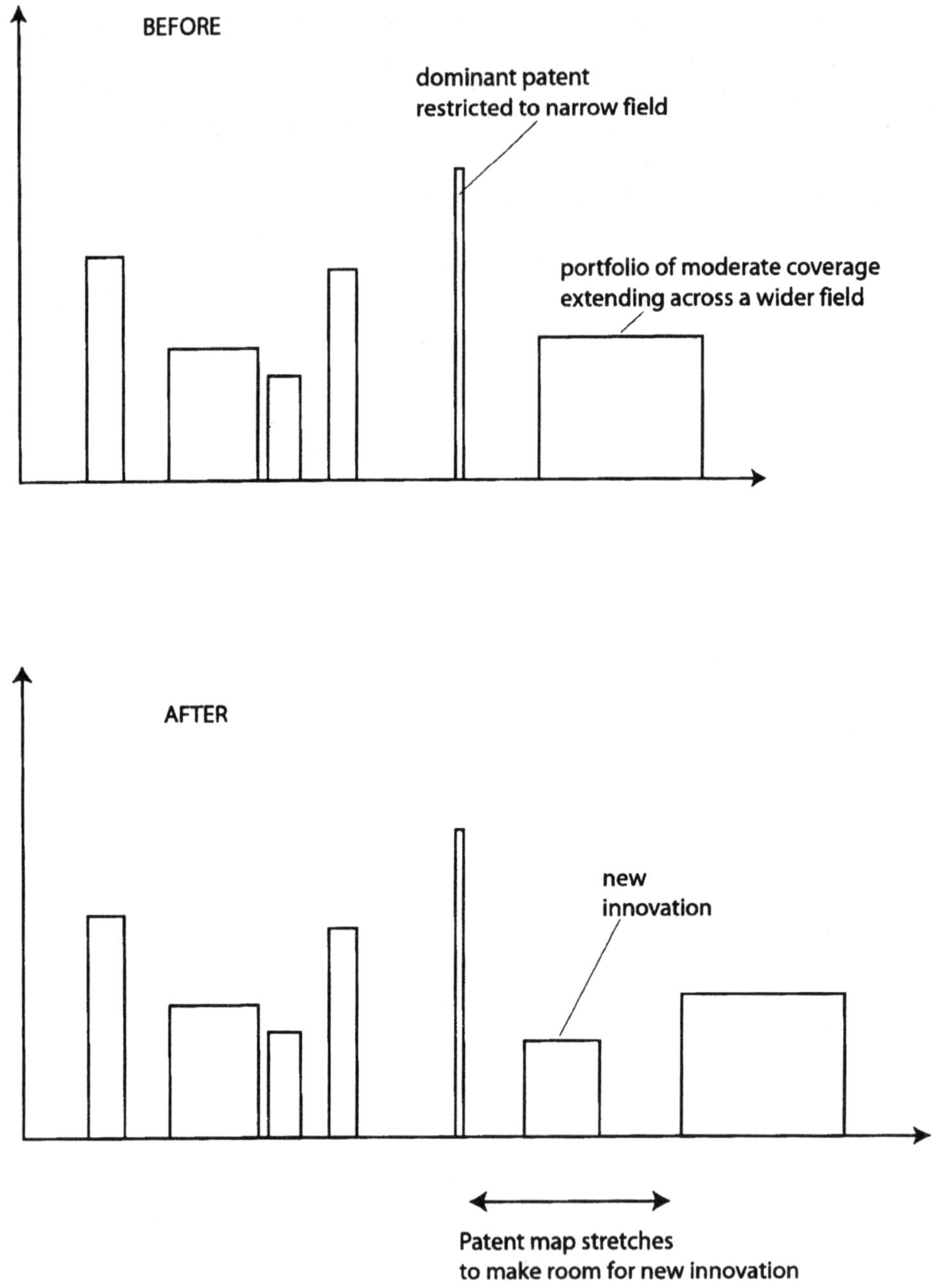

FIGURE 15–2.

[A] Whether the Courts Will Strictly Enforce Industry-Wide Licensing Programs

Industry-wide patent licensing policies, such as the W3C Royalty-Free Patent Policy, are designed to create royalty-free licenses under "essential claims" by default. If the owner of a patent containing "essential claims" does not take timely action to exclude the patent, the owner grants the industry a license. In some respects these license agreements are structured like shrink-wrap licenses and other contracts of adhesion. The terms take effect automatically, unless the party takes specific action to prevent it.

Of course, these license agreements are different from shrink-wrap licenses in that the parties have considerably more legal sophistication. It is therefore likely that courts will consider W3C members bound by the terms of the Patent Policy, once it is fully adopted. Counsel who represent W3C member clients therefore need to be mindful of the W3C Patent Policy and take steps to ensure that their clients comply.

TABLE OF CASES

References are to sections.

INDEX

References are to sections.